Preface

This series, intended for use in college courses and at G.C.E. Advanced level, seeks actively to involve students with historical evidence. Each book provides a wealth of contemporary material for study; this material will not only illustrate many aspects of the period under study, but will also face students with some of the problems which begin to arise whenever original source material is used.

In each book questions are posed which are basic to the period concerned. The documents which follow are intended to be read with the questions in mind, and they will begin to suggest possible answers. Inevitably, they will also confront the reader with many further questions, with apparent contradictions, with problems of bias, of lack of clarity, and of interpretation – in short, with the complexity of historical judgments. The student should thus gain insights into the period under study, into the type of original material available for the study, and into the task of the historian.

This volume deals with the particular problems faced by the last Tory Governments of 1812–1830 and with the leading political personalities of the period.

Stephen R. Gibbons
Stanley J. Houston
General Editors

Contents

THE AGE OF LORD LIVERPOOL

PHILIP REVILL

O27·1·94

EVIDENCE IN
HISTORY
Blackie

£2·05

EVIDENCE IN
HISTORY

GENERAL EDITORS

Stephen R. Gibbons
Head of Combined Studies
College of Sarum St Michael
Salisbury

Stanley J. Houston
Head of History
King's College School
Wimbledon

ISBN 0 216 90739 X

PUBLISHED BY
Blackie & Son Ltd
Bishopbriggs, Glasgow G64 2NZ
Furnival House, 14–18 High Holborn, London WC1V 6BX

PRINTED IN GREAT BRITAIN BY
Robert MacLehose & Co. Ltd, Printers to the University of Glasgow

Introduction 1

An old, mad, blind, despised and dying king, –
Princes, the dregs of their dull race, who flow
Through public scorn – mud from a muddy spring, –
Rulers who neither see, nor feel, nor know,
But leech-like to their fainting country cling,
Till they drop, blind in blood, without a blow, –
A people starved and stabbed in the untilled field, –
An army which liberticide and prey
Makes as a two-edged sword to all who wield, –
Golden and sanguine laws which tempt and slay;
Religion Christless, Godless – a book sealed;
A Senate, – Time's worst statute unrepealed, –
Are graves, from which a glorious phantom may
Burst, to illumine our tempestuous day.

POETICAL WORKS
by P.B. Shelley   O.U.P., 1919   *p.570*

The great Tory ministry which ... governed England for above
twenty years with unbroken success and unequalled glory.
THE LIFE OF LORD LIVERPOOL, vol. I
by C.D. Yonge   Macmillan, 1868   *p.229*

Can Shelley's view of England in 1819 and the estimate of Lord
Liverpool's first biographer refer to the same group of men? The
contrast of left- and right-wing interpretations of this controversial
period has continued to the present day – compare, for example, the
works of Cookson and Thompson listed in the Further Reading section
– and it remains difficult even after a hundred and fifty years to exclude
political bias from any judgment on the last Tory Governments.

How 'reactionary' we consider the Ministry up to 1820, and how
'liberal' thereafter (though there is a tendency among modern
historians and recent writers on this period to blur the distinction
between the two traditionally contrasted parts of Liverpool's Premiership), will depend not only on the point of view with which we
start, but also on how we define 'reactionary' and 'liberal'. Whether or

not we consider the policies of the Governments of these years to have been justifiable or successful will depend on whether we see our task as students of history to be simply to understand why men acted as they did, or further, to judge whether they could or should have acted differently. Is to understand all to forgive all? To change the cliché, if politics is the art of the possible, we must seek to understand the constraints, both physical and mental, within which the politicians of the time operated: to see what they *could* do, and also what they thought they *should* do. This selection of primary and secondary sources seeks to provide some evidence on which to judge the men who governed England under George IV, their opponents, and their policies. In concentrating on certain key men and issues, it inevitably omits many important aspects of the period, which the student who wishes to probe deeper should go on to investigate.

In particular, the main trends of thought in the early nineteenth century should be considered: democratic ideas such as those of Tom Paine in *The Rights of Man*, and the conservatism of Edmund Burke; the *laissez faire* and free trade economic theories of Adam Smith, Thomas Malthus and David Ricardo; the 'philosophic radicalism' of Jeremy Bentham and James Mill; the socialist Utopia preached by Robert Owen; the evangelical Christianity of men like William Wilberforce and Thomas Fowell Buxton; and not least, the odd bundle of ideas, defying categorization, propounded by William Cobbett, who is only briefly represented here. Secondly, the economic and social background needs to be thoroughly understood if the politics are to be fairly judged, since the politicians were having to grapple with novel and complex problems posed by the rapid pace of industrial and agricultural change. Thirdly, other important contemporary issues (the abolition of slavery, the reform of the Poor Law, the introduction of general elementary education, the development of effective factory legislation and, above all, the reform of Parliament itself), which are omitted from this book only because no conclusion or decision was reached by 1830, should be remembered. Perhaps, indeed, the Tories should be judged on what they failed to do as well as on what they did, as the final pages of this book suggest; but no government, even in the late twentieth century, can do everything.

> Belayed by their conservative principles, they proceeded with great caution and great thoroughness, and though their achievements were not spectacular they had a solidity which was not always present in the great Whig reforms of the 1830s. Certainly the least that can be said of such a strategy is that in their own time as the lessees of power, Liverpool and his colleagues had no reason to think that it had failed.

LORD LIVERPOOL'S ADMINISTRATION 1815–1822
by J.E. Cookson   Scottish Academic Press, 1975   *p.401*

Tories, Whigs and Radicals

▬▬▬▬▬▬▬▬▬▬▬▬▬▬▬▬▬▬

Before examining the particular problems faced by the Tory Governments, it is necessary to assess the quality of the leading ministers and
the strength of the opposition which they faced, together with some of
the general difficulties of government in the early nineteenth century.
The Liverpool Administration emerged from the political crisis
following the assassination of Spencer Perceval in May 1812; it was a
slightly reconstructed continuation of the previous Ministry and was
not expected to last long.

Stuart Wortley's Motion, passed in the House of Commons on 21 May
1812:

> It was notorious that an administration was now upon the eve of
> being formed, which no disinterested man thought adequate to
> meet the exigencies of the times.... If the present government
> were not very strong, even with the aid of Mr. Perceval's great
> talents, they were certainly worse than weak without them.... He
> was anxious to see an administration formed upon a liberal basis,
> calculated to comprehend the talents and influence of the country,
> and to promote its security and honour.
>
> PARLIAMENTARY DEBATES, *1st Series, vol.23, (1812) cols.249–252*

What overall judgments have been made about this Administration?

> From this unpromising beginning, it became a powerful, success-
> ful Ministry, and permanent, with but two exceptions, beyond all
> former example. It terminated with unprecedented success and
> glory the greatest war in which the country had ever been engaged.
> ... The return of peace and the inevitable reaction brought with it
> domestic dangers almost as violent, almost as enduring, as the war
> itself. These also it surmounted, and, amid circumstances of great
> and universal financial distress, laid the foundation of that great
> and wonderful commercial prosperity which for the last forty years
> has been the most distinguishing feature of our national history.

Such achievements and results supersede the necessity of panegyric.

THE LIFE OF LORD LIVERPOOL, vol. I
by C.D. Yonge   Macmillan, 1868 *p.427*

Having arrogated to itself the name of an illustrious historical party, it pursued a policy which was either founded on no principle whatever, or on principles exactly contrary to those which had always guided the conduct of the great Tory leaders. The chief members of this official confederacy were men distinguished by none of the conspicuous qualities of statesmen. They had none of the divine gifts that govern senates and guide councils. They were not orators; they were not men of deep thought or happy resource, or of penetrative and sagacious minds. Their political ken was essentially dull and contracted. They expended some energy in obtaining a defective, blundering acquaintance with foreign affairs; they knew as little of the real state of their own country as savages of an approaching eclipse.

CONINGSBY
by Benjamin Disraeli (first pub. 1844)   Peter Davies, 1927   pp.70–71

Probably no English government has ever been quite so near, in spirit and licence, to the atmosphere that we used to associate with the Tsar's government of Russia as the Government that ruled England for the first few years of the peace.

THE SKILLED LABOURER 1760–1832
by J.L. and B. Hammond (first pub. 1917)   Longmans, 1932 *p.371*

The most frequently encountered interpretation of British politics between Waterloo and Canning's return to power is that of a reactionary government under increasing pressure from outside suddenly making good by bringing in men of more liberal inclination .... In fact, Liverpool's administration was neither reactionary nor suddenly reformist in 1822.... The charge of 'reaction' levelled against Liverpool and his colleagues is usually based, following the example of the Victorian 'Whig' historians, on their opposition to those popular forces which were eventually triumphant. What it overlooks is that, on the whole, they managed to keep the support of those popular forces which were triumphant in the immediate future. Indeed they were not reactionary.... They reformed, albeit slowly and cautiously ....

It is not difficult to argue that the pace of 'improvement' would have been more rapid but for the ministers themselves .... Having regard only to the administrative equipment at their disposal,

there seems to be no reason why Lord Liverpool and his ministers
could not have done what the Whigs did ten years after them.

LORD LIVERPOOL'S ADMINISTRATION 1815–1822

by J.E. Cookson   Scottish Academic Press, 1975   *pp.395–400*

How effective was the Government's control of Parliament and the country?

The following table shows how far there was a straight two-party
system in this period. Totals exclude M.P.s with no voting record, but
include those returned at by-elections.

	Government	Government fringe	Waverers	Opposition fringe	Opposition	Total
1812–1818	253	78	102	83	149	665
1818–1820	261	80	48	16	171	576
1820–1826	250	99	114	66	154	683

THE WHIGS IN OPPOSITION 1815–1830

by A. Mitchell   O.U.P., 1967   *p.66*

Oldfield's analysis of electoral patronage in 1816 (England and Wales):

Returned by	Peers by nomination	by influence	Commoners by nomination	by influence	The Treasury etc.
No. of M.P.s	115	103	85	52	16

ENGLISH HISTORICAL DOCUMENTS, vol.11 (1783–1832)

edited by A. Aspinall and E.A. Smith   Eyre & Spottiswoode, 1959

p.236

An estimate by the Tory Secretary to the Admiralty, 1827:
Number of members returned to the House of Commons by the
influence of some of the peers ... Total 203, in the hands of what
may be called the Tory aristocracy. The Whig seats are about 73.

CORRESPONDENCE AND DIARIES OF JOHN WILSON CROKER, vol.1

edited by L.J. Jennings   Murray, 1884   *pp.368, 372*

The difficulty of managing the House of Commons, 1819:
The Lord Chancellor ascribes the defeat of last night ... to the
heretofore example of supineness in the official attendance [i.e.
members of the Government] which disquieted the independent
members, and a general want of energy in the House of Commons
by which the Opposition has been allowed to originate every
motion and to have got possession of the Committees upon the
main questions now under consideration. Lord Sidmouth admitted that there was a waywardness in the friends and supporters of
the Government which rendered the conduct of the public
business extremely arduous and doubtful.

THE LETTERS OF GEORGE IV 1812–1830, vol. 2

edited by A. Aspinall   C.U.P., 1938   *p.288*

6

The "System" that "Works so Well"!! - or The Boroughmongers GRINDING Machine.

Although published during the Reform crisis of 1831, this Cruikshank cartoon satirizes the system which helped to keep the Tories in power for so long. Notice the names of rotten boroughs on the mill-wheel; the mill, supported on the cannon and muskets of the Army, represents the House of Commons.

The greatest source of Government weakness was that there was not a ministerial group sufficiently strong to guarantee safe divisions. ... The Government was severely limited in the control which it could exercise over members, yet to the majority of members the continuance of the Tory Government was of the first importance. ... If the Government forbore from putting pressure upon its supporters, it might be expected that it would take steps to see that they were well informed of the Government's intentions. But party meetings were few, and held only when the Government had particularly unpopular measures to propose. ... The impression ... is that of men often at their wits' end to know how to carry on the day-to-day business in the House of Commons, frequently at the mercy of a capricious independent vote, and realising but slowly that their methods were ill-adapted to the needs of the time.

LORD LIVERPOOL AND LIBERAL TORYISM
by W.R. Brock   C.U.P., 1941   *pp.85, 101–105*

The independent members, backbench M.P.s who were mainly country gentlemen, were a major problem for any government.

Henry Bankes spoke for the independent members in the Commons:

Himself and his hon. friends near him had as little inclination as any set of men in that House to support a mere party measure; it made as little difference to him as to other gentlemen what individuals formed the administration of the country. As long as he had the honour of a seat in that House, so long he should be always ready to support them, while they appeared to him to act compatible with the great interests of the country.

PARLIAMENTARY DEBATES, *2nd Series, vol. 4, (1821) col. 392*

A modern historian stresses the lack of administrative machinery then:

At the head of the system [of internal government], if system it may just be called, was the Home Office.... It was both understaffed and undistinguished. In the year 1812, when it was taken over by Lord Sidmouth, *The Times* described it as 'the sink of all the imbecility attached to every ministry for the last thirty years'.... The Home Office had correspondents but no servants or agents in the provinces. The peace-keeping machinery of the country in 1812 was almost precisely what it had been in 1588. There was a small, quasi-official police-force in London. Outside London, all that existed was amateur, voluntary and unpaid.... Without the willing and able activity of the Lord Lieutenant, the Justice of the Peace, and the self-organised and self-ordered citizens of the towns, the Home Office – and the Government as a whole – would have been either paralysed or compelled to resort to military rule. ... The remarkable fact is not that England of the Regency experienced considerable disorder, but that she did not experience a great deal more of it.

WATERLOO TO PETERLOO
by R.J. White   Penguin, 1968   *pp.115–117*

King George IV was a major problem for his ministers, and often an obstacle to their wishes, from the time he became Regent in 1811.

He had few public virtues to compensate for the offensiveness of his private example. His duties to the State – the mere routine of the Kingly office – were invariably performed with tardiness and reluctance. Without any strength of character but that which proceeded from his irresistible craving for ease and indulgence, his best qualities were distorted into effeminate vices. The constitutional bravery of his house forsook him, and he became a moral coward, whom his official servants had to govern as a petted child.

HISTORY OF THE THIRTY YEARS PEACE 1816–1846, vol. 1
by Harriet Martineau (first pub. 1858)   Bell, 1877   *p.34*

The Prince Regent in Garter Robes by Sir Thomas Lawrence; reproduced by gracious permission of Her Majesty the Queen. The 'official' portraits which follow are all by Lawrence except where stated; as historical evidence they should be compared wherever possible with the cartoonist's view of the same subject.

George's extravagance was a severe embarrassment to a Government under pressure to reduce taxation and expenditure at a time of economic depression.

One M.P. hoped the House 'would hear no more of that squanderous and lavish profusion which in a certain quarter resembled more the pomp and magnificence of a Persian satrap

The Radical View of the Prince Regent, by George Cruikshank, from The
Political House that Jack Built *published by William Hone in 1819.*

    This is THE MAN − *all shaven and shorn,*
    All cover'd with Orders − and all forlorn;
    THE DANDY OF SIXTY, *who bows with a grace,*
    And has taste in wigs, collars, cuirasses and lace;
    Who, to tricksters, and fools, leaves the State and its treasure,
    And, when Britain's in tears, sails about at his pleasure. . . .

seated in all the splendour of oriental state, than the sober dignity of a British prince, seated in the bosom of his subjects. He hoped, too, that they should hear no more of expenditure on thatched cottages that were hardly fit for princes.'

THE LIFE OF LORD LIVERPOOL, vol.2
by C.D. Yonge   Macmillan, 1868   *p.268*

The reference is to the Royal Pavilion at Brighton and the Royal Lodge at Windsor.

The King frequently threatened to dismiss his ministers, and influenced the composition of the Cabinet, for example excluding Canning for over a year until 1822.

> [The King] began to complain of Lord Liverpool. He says he cannot go on with him, and that he will not; ... that if the Cabinet chose to stand or fall with Lord L. they must fall; if not, he does not wish for any further change.... Lord Liverpool was captious, jealous, and impracticable; he objects to everything, and even when he gives way, which is nine times in ten, he does it with so bad a grace that it is worse than an absolute refusal.

CORRESPONDENCE AND DIARIES OF JOHN WILSON CROKER, vol.1
edited by L.J. Jennings   Murray, 1884   *p.198*

This was in July 1821; the King's anger was due to Liverpool's handling of the affair of Queen Caroline in the previous year and to his attempts to strengthen the Government by restoring Canning to office. Even after Castlereagh's suicide had made the latter move essential, George wrote to the Prime Minister opposing it; it was Wellington who persuaded him to give way.

> The King has been much surprised by Lord Liverpool's proposition relative to Mr. Canning.... If there be no alternative, the King takes for granted that Lord Liverpool and the other members of the Cabinet are prepared to break up the Government.

THE LETTERS OF GEORGE IV 1812–1830, vol.2
edited by A. Aspinall   C.U.P., 1938   *p.535*

Even the Duke of Wellington had great difficulty in persuading the King to agree to Catholic Emancipation in 1829.

> The King talked for six hours. The Duke says he never witnessed a more painful scene. He was so evidently insane .... The King objected to every part of the Bill. He would not hear it.... A quarter of an hour after he [the Duke] got home ... he received a letter from the King declaring that to avoid the *mischief of having no Administration* he consented to the Bill proceeding as a measure of Government, but with infinite pain.

LORD ELLENBOROUGH'S POLITICAL DIARY, vol.1 (1828–1830)
edited by Lord Colchester   Bentley, 1881   *pp.376–379*

Lord Liverpool

What was the calibre of the leading Tory ministers?

Robert Banks Jenkinson, second Earl of Liverpool, was Prime Minister from 1812–1827, longer than any man since.

As a minister, Lord Liverpool may perhaps be admitted not to have been distinguished by any striking originality of views or rapid fertility of resource; but he possessed qualities, if less showy, more valuable and better calculated to carry a nation with wide and complicated interests in safety through periods of difficulty and peril. . . . His natural acuteness was sharpened and strengthened by most extensive information on every subject which could affect the deliberations of an English Cabinet. . . .

Even of his bitterest opponents none ever questioned his unsullied integrity, his undeviating freedom from jobbery of every kind, his rare scrupulousness in the distribution of his patronage, particularly of the ecclesiastical preferments in his gift; his perfect disinterestedness, displayed in the fact that he left office a poorer man than he had entered on it. . . .

THE LIFE OF LORD LIVERPOOL, vol.3
by C.D. Yonge   Macmillan, 1868   *pp.457–458*

The Arch-Mediocrity who presided, rather than ruled, over this Cabinet of Mediocrities . . . had himself some glimmering traditions of political science. . . . In a subordinate position his meagre diligence and his frigid method might not have been without value; but the qualities that he possessed were misplaced; nor can any character be conceived less invested with the happy properties of a leader. In the conduct of public affairs his disposition was exactly the reverse of that which is the characteristic of great men. He was peremptory in little questions, and great ones he left open.

CONINGSBY
by Benjamin Disraeli (first pub. 1844)   Peter Davies, 1927   pp.75–76

To his public life he brought qualities which, in aggregate, few prime ministers have equalled. In grasp of principles, mastery of detail, discernment of means, and judgement of individuals he was almost faultless. Cautious and unhurried in weighing a situation, he was prompt and decisive when the time came for action. In debate he was not only informed, lucid and objective, but conspicuously honest. . . . He never dismissed a minister; he was never ungrateful or disloyal. Kind by temperament, he had an instinctive tact in dealing with others. His conciliatory manner smoothed away innumerable personal difficulties. He was a man whom it was almost impossible to dislike. . . .

"And when Ahithophel saw that his Councel was not followed, he saddled his Ass, & arose & went & hanged himself &c."

'*Ahithophel in the Dumps*', *a reference to the Old Testament adviser of King David. This cartoon is interesting as a comment on Liverpool's position after the trial of Queen Caroline, and for comparison with the official portrait of Liverpool by Lawrence.*

Liverpool was never a mere chairman presiding over a Cabinet of superior talents. ... It is clear that the guiding lines of policy were always firmly in Liverpool's hands, in consultation with an inner ring of ministers.... Liverpool himself kept a close supervision of all the main departments, including the Foreign Office; and in matters of trade and finance was always the dominating figure. ...

Liverpool was a conservative statesman in the fundamental sense. He wished to avoid organic change by pursuing administrative reform. But he was neither a bigot nor a reactionary. ... The more the nineteenth century is put into perspective, the more significant does Liverpool's role appear. It was not merely that his political skill had kept an administration together so long or that his sheer professionalism as an administrator had enabled him to master all the diverse needs of government between 1812 and 1827. Even more important is that in the face of enormous practical difficulties he opened up the road along which early Victorian Britain was to travel with increasing certainty and profit in the next generation.

Asa Briggs in THE PRIME MINISTERS, VOL. I
edited by H. van Thal   Allen & Unwin, 1974   *pp.287–296*

Liverpool to Wellington, 1812:

> I can assure you I never sought the situation in which I find myself
> now placed; but having accepted it from a sense of public duty, I
> am determined to do my utmost for the service of the Prince
> Regent as long as I have reason to believe that I possess his
> confidence.

SUPPLEMENTARY DESPATCHES AND MEMORANDA OF THE DUKE OF
WELLINGTON, vol.7

edited by the 2nd Duke of Wellington   Kraus Reprint Co., N.Y., 1973

p.402

Huskisson wrote to his wife in 1819 of the nervous anxiety of Liverpool
('Old Mouldy') over the problem of whether to restore the Gold
Standard:

> Between ourselves, the Government are very much embarrassed
> what to do, and will not, I apprehend, have the best of it. However,
> for this, as for many other scrapes, they may thank the genius of
> Old Mouldy. Liverpool is in one of his grand fidgetts. Yesterday he
> said if Tierney [Whig leader in the Commons] were to beat us, it
> would be fatal, if not to the whole Government at least to the
> Treasury – at least, he added, I do not see how I could remain at
> the head of that Department.

British Museum Add. MSS. 38949 f.38

Mrs Arbuthnot, wife of one of Liverpool's colleagues, did not like him.
She wrote of his difficulties with the King in 1821:

> Lord Liverpool is in a great fuss, frightened to death lest his
> colleagues should desert, so that all his threats of resigning and
> desire to retire from office end in smoke. I never thought he meant
> to go; but it is quite childish, a man so repeatedly saying he wishes
> to go and then ending by sticking like a leach to his place. . . .
>
> Lord Liverpool has a disagreeable, cold manner and a most
> querulous, irritable temper, which render it a difficult and an
> unpleasant task to act in public life with him; but he is a most
> upright, honest, excellent man, conscientiously devoted to the
> service and to the real good of his country.

MRS ARBUTHNOT'S JOURNAL, vol.1

edited by Francis Bamford and the Duke of Wellington   Macmillan, 1950

pp.117, 121

Robert Stewart, Viscount Castlereagh, as Foreign Secretary and Leader
of the House of Commons from 1812 until his suicide in 1822, attracted
most of the Government's unpopularity upon his own head. Byron was
particularly vicious:

Viscount Castlereagh

Cold-blooded, smooth-faced, placid miscreant
  Dabbling its sleek young hands in Erin's gore,
And thus for wider carnage taught to pant,
  Transferred to gorge upon a sister shore
The vulgarest tool that Tyranny could want,
  With just enough of talent, and no more,
To lengthen fetters by another fixed,
  And offer poison long already mixed.

THE DEDICATION TO DON JUAN
by Lord Byron

Thomas Creevey, a Whig M.P., wrote grudgingly after Castlereagh's death:

Death settles a fellow's reputation in no time, and now that
Castlereagh is dead, I defy any human being to discover a single
feature of his character that can stand a moment's criticism. By
experience, good manners and great courage, he managed a
corrupt House of Commons pretty well, with some address. This
is the whole of his intellectual merit. He had a limited understand-
ing and no knowledge, and his whole life was spent in an avowed,
cold-blooded contempt of every honest public principle. A worse,
or, if he had had talent and ambition for it, a more dangerous,
public man never existed.

THE CREEVEY PAPERS, vol.2
edited by Sir Herbert Maxwell   Murray, 1903   *p.42*

He managed the foreign affairs of the country with a judgement
and ability that will hand down his name with honour to posterity,
when those of his pitiful revilers will be buried in oblivion. He had
a natural slowness of constitution of which he was himself quite
aware, for he has often told me he required the goading and
violence of the House of Commons to rouse him, and that he was
determined never to go into the House of Lords as they were too
quiet and sleepy for him. The consequences of this temperament,
and of his not having had a classical education, which rendered his
language involved and often incorrect, were that, when he had to
make a statement or an opening speech, he was generally flat and
dull and scarcely commanded the attention of the House; but in
reply, and particularly when the Opposition had been violent or
ungentlemanlike, he was very powerful. Nothing, too, could
exceed his tact and judgement in dwelling on the strong points of
his own arguments or the weak ones of his antagonists; and his
management was so good, and he was himself so gentlemanlike and
so high minded, that he was one of the most popular leaders the
Government ever had.

MRS ARBUTHNOT'S JOURNAL, vol.1
edited by Francis Bamford and the Duke of Wellington   Macmillan, 1950
pp.181–182

So dominant was Castlereagh's personality in the Commons that
many Radical critics regarded Liverpool's Administration as in
many ways Castlereagh's Government. This did scant justice to
the skill and intelligence of Liverpool, but it helps to explain why
Castlereagh became so hated. He had to defend measures such as
the suspension of Habeas Corpus and the Six Acts, as well as
damping down criticism of the magistrates after the Peterloo affair
in 1819. ...

Castlereagh's attitudes to the issues of the day were not
obscurantist. ... He was prepared to condone the cautious

disfranchisement of boroughs which were guilty of excessive or notorious malpractices or corruption.... Throughout his career Castlereagh was sympathetic to Catholic relief.... In economic and financial matters he had always been identified with the more liberal section of Liverpool's Cabinet. ... Had he lived he might well have been associated more publicly and more prominently with the more liberal period of Tory rule in the 1820s.... Castlereagh's appeal was to all sections of the Tory party, and he would have been a good choice to succeed Liverpool as Prime Minister.

CASTLEREAGH
by J.W. Derry   Allen Lane, 1976   *pp.220–221, 20–21, 24*

The leading reactionaries in the Cabinet were *Henry Addington, Viscount Sidmouth*, who was Home Secretary from 1812 until 1821 and remained in the Cabinet at George IV's wish until 1824; and *John Scott, Earl of Eldon*, Lord Chancellor from 1801–1806 and 1807–1828. Both were of middle-class origin.

Viscount Sidmouth by G. Richmond

Samuel Bamford, a Radical weaver from Lancashire, was examined before the Privy Council in 1817, and was pleasantly surprised to find Sidmouth human:

The person who addressed me was a tall, square and bony figure, upwards of fifty years of age, I should suppose; and with thin and rather grey hair; his forehead was broad and prominent, and from their cavernous orbits looked mild and intelligent eyes. His manner was affable, and much more encouraging to freedom of speech than I had expected.

THE AUTOBIOGRAPHY OF SAMUEL BAMFORD, vol.2 (PASSAGES IN THE LIFE OF A RADICAL)

by Samuel Bamford (first pub. 1839)   Cass, 1967   *p.106*

Addington was almost as convinced a reactionary as he has been depicted. His talents were in no way extraordinary. On almost every controversial issue of the day he was to be found securely entrenched on the wrong side. Yet I am left in no doubt that he has been monstrously misused by history. As a Minister he was responsible, conscientious and far from ineffectual. As a man he was kindly, courteous and sincere. His honour and his integrity would be remarkable in any age and any profession. . . .

As Home Secretary he was violently controversial; the champion of reaction against progress, or, seen from another angle, of authority against anarchy. . . . I would have felt no serious qualms in depicting Addington as an ogre, a man as outrageous as many of the laws he enforced. That I do not is because the evidence is simply not there. On the contrary, Addington emerges as a good man, doing his best to administer an ill-judged policy with charity,

Lord Eldon

Lawrence's portrait of Lord Eldon should be compared to William Heath's cartoon of 1826. 'Paul Pry' (the leading character in a popular play of the time) is seen visiting the Court of Chancery. Eldon's clinging to office, the delays and abuses of Chancery (notice the mountains of documents and cases awaiting action), his wealth, patronage and financial meanness are all attacked here.

humanity and, above all, absolute fairness. His limitations were obvious in all that he did: it is unjust that only these should be remembered and his considerable virtues forgotten.

ADDINGTON

by Philip Ziegler   Collins, 1965   *pp.11–12*

Lord Eldon has one of the best-natured faces in the world; it is pleasant to meet him in the street, plodding along with an umbrella under his arm, without one trace of pride, of spleen, or discontent in his whole demeanour, void of offence, with almost rustic simplicity and honesty of appearance – a man that makes friends at first sight, and could hardly make enemies, if he would; and whose only fault is that he cannot say *Nay* to power, or subject himself to an unkind word or look from a King or a Minister. He is a thoroughbred Tory.... There has been no stretch of power attempted in his time that he has not seconded: no existing abuse so odious or so absurd, that he has not sanctioned it. He has gone the whole length of the most unpopular designs of Ministers . . . .

On all the great questions that have divided party opinion or agitated the public mind, the Chancellor has been found uniformly and without a single exception on the side of prerogative and power, and against every proposal for the advancement of freedom.

THE SPIRIT OF THE AGE
by William Hazlitt (first pub. 1825)   Collins, 1969   pp.236–237

It should be remembered that all of the 'liberal Tories' of the 1820s, and also Wellington, had held office at some time between 1812 and 1820 as well. *George Canning* was President of the Board of Control for India from 1816–1820, Foreign Secretary and Leader of the Commons from 1822–1827, and then Prime Minister for 100 days until his death.

George Canning by Sir Thomas Lawrence and R. Evans

Europe lost in him the ablest statesman, and the Commons of England the finest orator of his day. . . . As a practical statesman, his views were always clear and manly. He was the most unyielding opponent of all the schemes which, for more than thirty years, had thrown the world into confusion under the name of reform: and he had done his country much good service in maintaining the integrity of her existing institutions. . . . The later acts of his public life, before he became Prime Minister, had, in an equal manner, strengthened his hold on the admiration and favour of his country.

On the other hand, it is true that there were circumstances which prevented a large and influential portion of the people from

A Radical Caricature of Sidmouth, Castlereagh and Canning, by George Cruikshank, from The Political House that Jack Built.

> *This is* THE DOCTOR *of Circular fame,*
> *A Driv'ller, a Bigot, a Knave without shame:*
> *And that's* DERRY DOWN TRIANGLE *by name,*
> *From the Land of misrule, and half-hanging, and flame:*
> *And that is* THE SPOUTER OF FROTH BY THE HOUR,
> *The worthless colleague of their infamous power. . . .*

giving him as much of their confidence as they willingly gave him of their admiration. There were parts of his public life in which his steadiness of purpose and consistency of conduct might be questioned; there were others in which it might be doubted whether perfect good faith to his fellow-labourers had not been sacrificed to ambition, and the last act of his life, that coalition, by which he chose to be first, through the support of former opponents, rather than to remain second in name among former friends, was more than questionable.

THE ANNUAL REGISTER, vol. 69   *1827*   *pp.190–191*

If the reader has paid public attention to the public efforts of Mr. Canning, he will find, that those efforts have had but one principal object in view: namely, to *prevent any change in the system*, by which the country has been governed for many years past. This is *all*, which he, as a statesman, appears to have thought worthy of his serious attention. . . . Castlereagh, fool as he was, almost downright idiot as he was, was much fitter for the present state of things than the really accomplished Mr Canning. . . . After all his hostility towards me, I am ready to acknowledge the greatness of his talents; I do not impute to him base selfishness or wicked intentions of any sort. I impute to him dangerous and destructive error, and from the effect of that error I wish to see the country delivered.

COBBETT'S POLITICAL REGISTER, 12 October 1822

Robert Peel had been Irish Secretary from 1812–1818, when still under thirty, and was Home Secretary from 1821–1827 and 1828–1830 as well as Leader of the Commons in the last two years.

Charles Williams-Wynn, M.P., to his patron Lord Grenville, 1820:

His irritability and a certain degree of arrogance which the want of family and connection renders less tolerable, have during the last two years rendered the House (particularly the ministerial men) less favourably disposed to him, but still he combines advantages of general character in the country, of talents and habits of business which altogether place him higher than any other man in the House.

LORD LIVERPOOL'S ADMINISTRATION 1815–1822
by J.E. Cookson   Scottish Academic Press, 1975   *p.291*

No man has come so near our definition of a constitutional statesman, – the powers of a first-rate man and the creed of a second-rate man. From a certain peculiarity of intellect and fortune, he was never in advance of his time. Of almost all the great measures with which his name is associated, he attained great eminence as an opponent before he attained even greater eminence as their advocate. On the Corn Laws, on the currency, on the amelioration of the criminal code, on Catholic emancipation . . . he was not one of the earliest labourers, or quickest converts. He did not bear the heat and burden of the day; other men laboured, and he entered into their labours.

THE COLLECTED WORKS OF WALTER BAGEHOT, vol.3
edited by Norman St. John Stevas   THE ECONOMIST, 1968, p.245

Mr. Peel is certainly the most unpopular leader a party can have. His low birth and vulgar manners would be not only forgiven but forgotten if he would practise the arts of conciliation, if he would be kind and gracious to those in office under him, and frank and good-natured to his supporters in Parliament; but, instead of that, nothing can exceed his arrogance and ill-temper.

MRS ARBUTHNOT'S JOURNAL, vol.2
edited by Francis Bamford and the Duke of Wellington   Macmillan, 1950
                                                                    p.187

Sir Robert Peel by John Linnell

William Huskisson, a 'Canningite', held minor office for many years before Canning secured him the Presidency of the Board of Trade in 1822, when *Frederick Robinson* left this post to become Chancellor of the Exchequer in place of Nicholas Vansittart, who was quietly retired with a peerage.

> Robinson is probably unequal to the present difficult conjuncture; a fair and candid man, and an excellent Minister in days of calm and sunshine, but not endowed with either capacity or experience for these stormy times, besides being disqualified for vigorous measures by the remissness and timidity of his character. . . . His mind is not sufficiently enlarged, nor does he have any distinct ideas upon the subject: he is fighting in the dark. Everybody knows that Huskisson is the real author of the finance measures of Government.
>
> THE GREVILLE MEMOIRS, vol. I
> *edited by Lytton Strachey and Roger Fulford, Macmillan, 1938 pp.156–157*

Greville's estimate of Huskisson after his death in the famous railway accident at the opening of the Liverpool and Manchester Railway in 1830:

> There is no man in Parliament, or perhaps out of it, so well versed in finance, commerce, trade and colonial matters, and he is therefore a very great and irreparable loss. It is nevertheless

remarkable that it is only within the last five or six years that he acquired the great reputation which he latterly enjoyed. I do not think he was looked upon as more than a second-rate man till his speeches on the silk trade and the shipping interest; but when he became President of the Board of Trade he devoted himself with indefatigable application to the maturing and reducing to practice those commercial improvements with which his name is associated, and to which he owes all his glory and most of his unpopularity. It is equally true that all the ablest men in the country coincide with him, and that the mass of the community are persuaded that his plans are mischievous to the last degree.

THE GREVILLE MEMOIRS, vol. 2
edited by Lytton Strachey and Roger Fulford   Macmillan, 1938 pp.47–48

William Huskisson by R. Rothwell

The Duke of Wellington was an influential figure throughout the period, a Cabinet member from 1819 as Master General of Ordnance until his refusal to serve under Canning, and Prime Minister from 1828–1830: the last true Tory one.

Greville, who knew the Duke well, gave an estimate after his fall in 1830:

His is one of those mixed characters which it is difficult to praise or blame without the risk of doing it more or less than justice. He has talents which the event has proved to be sufficient to make him the second (and, now that Napoleon is gone, the first) general of the age, but which could not make him a tolerable Minister. Confident, presumptuous, and dictatorial, but frank, open, and good-humoured, he contrived to rule in the Cabinet without mortifying his colleagues, and he has brought it to ruin without forfeiting their regard. Choosing with a very slender stock of knowledge to take upon himself the sole direction of every department of Government, he completely sank under the burden. Originally imbued with the principles of Lord Castlereagh and the Holy Alliance, he brought all those predilections with him into office. ... When he found that the cause he advocated was lost, the Duke turned suddenly round, and surrendered his opinions at discretion. ... He has not been thoroughly true to any principle or any party; he contrived to disgust and alienate his old friends and adherents without conciliating or attaching those whose measures he at the eleventh hour undertook to carry into execution. ...

Greville added in 1850:

He coveted power, but he was perfectly disinterested, a great patriot if ever there was one, and he was always animated by a strong and abiding sense of duty.

THE GREVILLE MEMOIRS, vol.2
edited by Lytton Strachey and Roger Fulford Macmillan, 1938 pp.78–81

He was a very human character, also a humane one – a man of generosity and magnanimity. ... Certainly his temperament was not ideal for a Prime Minister, though it might not be easy to say what temperament is. The Duke found it more difficult to deal with a Cabinet than a military staff. ... Wellington is usually considered as a reactionary ultra-Tory opposed to all change. This is far from being wholly true. The two major reforms which occurred in his administration, the new police force and Catholic emancipation, were causes which he had long favoured and were not forced on him despite himself.

THE DUKE IN POWER
by Robert Blake THE SUNDAY TIMES, 5 November 1972

How effective was the Whig opposition?

The Whigs had been out of office since 1783, except for the brief Ministry of All the Talents in 1806–1807, and had come to accept this situation as the norm.

Sir James Mackintosh on the Whig plight, 1815:

I do not regret the obloquy with which we have been loaded during the present session: it is a proof that we are following, though with unequal steps, the great men who have filled the same benches before us. It was their lot to devote themselves to a life of thankless and often unpopular opposition, with no stronger allurement to ambition than a chance of a few months of office in half a century, and with no greater inducement to virtue than the faint hope of limiting and mitigating evil; always certain that the merit would never be acknowledged, and generally obliged to seek for the best proof of their services in the scurrility with which they were reviled.

PARLIAMENTARY DEBATES, *1st Series, vol.30, (1815) col.896*

Squire Western to Thomas Creevey, 17 February 1816:

There is no superior *mind* amongst us; great power of speaking, faculty of perplexing, irritation and complaints, but no super-eminent power to strike out a line of policy, and to command the *confidence* of the country. Brougham has shown his powers rather successfully, and exhibits some prudence in his plans of attack; but I cannot discern that superiority of judgement and of view (if I may so express myself) which is the *grand* desideratum. Tierney is an expert, narrow and wrong as ever; Ponsonby as inefficient; Horner as sonorous and *eloquent*, I must say, but I *cannot* see anything in him, say what they will, though he certainly speaks powerfully.

THE CREEVEY PAPERS, VOL. I
edited by Sir Herbert Maxwell   Murray, 1903   *p.251*

Earl Grey, the Whig leader in the Lords, often failed to attend Parliament at all. Lord Holland pleaded with him in April 1820:

I foresee much mischief and the possibility of the party being destroyed ... not by a revolution but by a dissolution of all its parts. ... I do not like the prospect of seeing a party of which my uncle [Charles James Fox] was and you are the head crumble to pieces for want of exertion to keep it together.

THE WHIGS IN OPPOSITION
by A. Mitchell   O.U.P., 1967   *p.141*

Though the independent members were often angry with the Government, they were not eager to see the Whigs in office, and this limited the extent of revolt. Henry Bankes made clear why in 1821:

The opposition ... were pledged to a reform in parliament which the present circumstances of the country could not with safety allow, and he therefore viewed it with unqualified apprehension. Another question to which they were pledged was catholic emancipation ... if the opposition came into power, that ruinous measure which he deprecated would inevitably pass.... The opposition were bound to a complete change of the system of government.... He concluded by expressing his firm reliance upon the councils of his majesty's government, and reiterating his opinion, that in the dangerous circumstances of the country no administration could be found so well entitled to his support as the one at present existing. . . .

PARLIAMENTARY DEBATES, *2nd Series, vol.4, (1821) col.394*

Radicals, however, saw the Whigs differently, as William Hazlitt wrote in 1819:

A modern Whig is but the fag-end of a Tory. . . . So I cannot find out the different drift, so far as politics are concerned, of the *Quarterly* and *Edinburgh Reviews* [Tory and Whig respectively], which remind one of Opposition coaches, that raise a great dust or spatter one another with mud, but both travel the same road and arrive at the same destination.

ROMANTICISM AND THE SOCIAL ORDER
by R.W. Harris   Blandford, 1969   *p.58*

The degree of truth in this view is indicated by a letter of Grey to a Whig M.P. in October 1819, referring to Peterloo:

The line of policy which I shall feel it incumbent upon me to pursue, must place me in equal hostility to the Government on the one hand, and to the Radicals on the other. . . . I will not now go into an examination of the principle of Reform which is the only one that will be tolerated by the leaders of the Popular Party, or rather of the Mob, or of the means by which they are endeavouring to effect their object, which certainly is not Reform, but Revolution. But I will desire you to look at the men themselves who lead in this cause. Is there one among them with whom you would trust yourself in the dark?

British Museum Add. MSS. 30,109 fs.56ff.

What kind of challenge was presented by Radicalism?

Clearly there was little chance of an alliance of Whigs and Radicals; and since, apart from Sir Francis Burdett, hardly any Radicals managed to enter the Commons through the unreformed electoral system, the Radical movement had to seek to put pressure on the Government from outside Parliament by propaganda, demonstration, and the threat of violence. (See Part 3, "Crisis and Controversy".)

A typical Radical programme: resolutions passed by the Oldham Deputy Meeting of 7 June 1819:

First, – That in consequence of the high price of provisions, enormous rents, excessive taxes, scarcity of employment, and lowness of wages; millions of healthy and industriously disposed Englishmen, are reduced to the deepest distress. . . .

Third, – That the laws which regulate the importation of products, are a great cause of this insupportable distress: and a proof that the interest of a few Land Proprietors, preponderates in our Legislative Assemblies, over the interest of millions of labourers.

Fourth, – That these laws are calculated to enrich a few thousands of worthless families: and to reduce to pauperism, want and misery, millions of individuals, infinitely more useful to society. . . .

Eighth, – That if these Corn Laws and other restraints on the importation of agricultural products be not repealed, and Universal Suffrage, and Annual Parliament be not adopted to prevent their recurrence, of such restrictions, this Meeting is convinced, that the labouring part of the people of this country, cannot long preserve their existence: and if they must die, either by starvation, or in defence of their rights, they cannot hesitate to prefer the latter. . . .

PETERLOO
by Donald Read   M.U.P., 1958   *pp.216–217*

At this time [1816–1817] the writings of William Cobbett suddenly became of great authority; they were read on nearly every cottage hearth in the manufacturing districts. . . . He directed his readers to the true cause of their sufferings – misgovernment; and to its proper corrective – parliamentary reform. Riots soon became scarce. . . . Hampden clubs [organizations pressing for reform of Parliament] were now established. . . . The Labourers . . . became deliberate and systematic in their proceedings.

THE AUTOBIOGRAPHY OF SAMUEL BAMFORD, vol.2 (PASSAGES IN THE LIFE OF A RADICAL)
by Samuel Bamford (first pub. 1839)   Cass, 1967   *p.7*

I missed scarcely a week to inculcate the doctrine of absolute necessity to avoid all acts of violence of every sort, and to observe strict and real obedience to the laws. . . . I did more in the space of a month, to prevent depredations of this sort, than all the new penal laws, all the magistrates, and all the troops, had been able to do in seven years.

COBBETT'S POLITICAL REGISTER, *16 August 1817*

A Radical criticism of Cobbett:

He is too much for any single newspaper antagonist, 'lays waste' a city orator or Member of Parliament, and bears hard upon the Government itself. He is a kind of *fourth estate* in the politics of the country. . . . Mr. Cobbett speaks almost as well as he writes. The only time I ever saw him he seemed to me a very pleasant man: easy of access, affable, clear-headed, simple and mild in his manner,

A vivid comment of 1819 by George Cruikshank on the Ministry's fears of French-style revolution led by the Radicals. (Left to right), Castlereagh, Eldon and the Prince Regent flee in terror, while poor Liverpool is trampled under foot. Note the reference to Hunt (left).

deliberate and unruffled in his speech, though some of his expressions were not very qualified. . . . As a political partisan, no one can stand against him. With his brandished club, like Giant Despair in the *Pilgrim's Progress,* he knocks out their brains: and not only no individual, but no corrupt system, could hold out against his powerful and repeated attacks. But with the same weapon swung round like a flail, with which he levels his antagonists, he lays his friends low, and puts his own party *hors de combat.* . . .

Though he is not servile or mercenary, he is the victim of self-will. He must pull down and pull in pieces: it is not in his disposition to do otherwise. It is a pity; for with his great talents he might do great things, if he would go right forward to any useful object, make thorough-stitch work of any question, or join hand and heart with any principle. . . . Mr. Cobbett is great in attack, not in defence: he cannot fight an uphill battle. He will not bear the least punishing. If any one turns on him (which few people like to do) he immediately turns tail. . . .

THE SPIRIT OF THE AGE

by William Hazlitt (first pub. 1825)   *Collins, 1969*   *pp.244–257*

Henry Hunt, 'the Orator', is described by Francis Place, the Radical tailor, in 1816:

> Hunt has been with me. He is a pretty sample of an ignorant, turbulent, mischief-making fellow, a highly dangerous one in troubled times. ... I told Hunt it was miserable to see the avidity with which ... [he and his political friends] sought to cut each other's throats, and that it would require nothing more in days of turbulence, whenever they should arise, than for those who hate the people to stimulate them to destroy one another, which would be as easy as putting yeast to the dough to make it rise. ... Hunt says his mode of acting is to dash at good points, and to care for no one; that he will mix with no committee, or any party; he will act by himself; that he does not intend to affront anyone, but cares not who is offended.
>
> THE LIFE OF FRANCIS PLACE
> *by Graham Wallas   Allen & Unwin, 1917*   *pp.119–120*

The ambiguity in the exhortations of demagogues like Hunt is shown in his speech at the first Spa Fields meeting on 15 November 1816:

> He knew the superiority of mental over physical force; nor would he counsel any resort to the latter till the former had been found ineffectual. Before physical force was applied to, it was their duty to petition, to remonstrate, to call aloud for timely reformation. Those who resisted the just demands of the people were the real friends of confusion and bloodshed ... but if the fatal day should be destined to arrive, he assured them that if he knew anything of himself, he would not be found concealed behind a counter, or sheltering himself in the rear.
>
> THE MAKING OF THE ENGLISH WORKING CLASS
> *by E.P. Thompson   Penguin, 1968*   *p.685*

The volume and virulence of the Radical newspapers meant that the freedom of the press continued to be an important issue; the authorities were relatively unsuccessful in their attempts to silence them.

From a letter by an unknown writer, about 1818:

> The Constitution is shaken to its foundation by the license of the Press, and the licentiousness of the Press is incited and upheld by the only means prescribed by the laws for its control. ...
>
> There appears to me to be but one channel open to our security – a bold, steady, manly appeal from these innovations and breaches in the Constitution, to the sober sense of the country, a late but vigorous determination of adopting *preventive* measures, and Parliamentary interference for the purpose of enforcing existing laws; or if necessary of making new enactments to prevent the publication of *unstampt* journals. That there is nothing

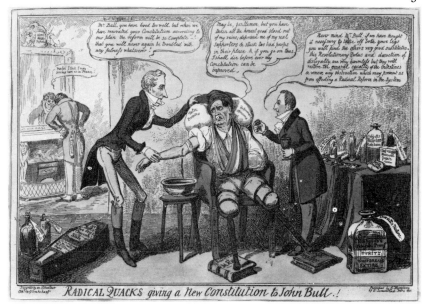

RADICAL QUACKS giving a New Constitution to John Bull..!

This cartoon, also by Cruikshank, should be compared with the previous one (see page 29). The 'Quacks' are Burdett (left) and Hobhouse. Note that John Bull's legs are in the coffin, labelled Church and State – his true supporters, while his wooden legs rest on the works of Tom Paine.

chimerical in the notions I have constantly entertained upon this subject may be inferred from the mere notoriety and popularity of men like Hone and Wooller [Radical journalists and publishers]. Had *preventive* measures been adopted a few months ago the public would not have known that such beings existed. By *penal prosecution* they are raised up and *armed* for any mischief to any extent they may think fit to carry it. . . .

Sedition and blasphemy are triumphant at a period in which the hands of Government are strengthened beyond the legitimate usage of the Constitution, overt acts are only *just* restrained within the strictest limits. If something be not done before the suspension be taken off what is to prevent the fearful encroachments of popular disaffection, heated by seditious harangues and drawn forth by new and *triumphant* leaders?

THE LETTERS OF GEORGE IV 1812–1830, vol.3

edited by A. Aspinall   C.U.P., 1938   *pp.492–494*

In 1815 the Government had increased the newspaper stamp duty to 4d. but had been unable to stem the flood of unstamped papers, such as

Cobbett's *Twopenny Trash*, which followed. In 1817 Hone was three times acquitted on charges of blasphemy against his parody *John Wilkes' Catechism*, from which the next extract is quoted:

The Ten Commandments

I	Thou shalt have no other Patron but me.
II	Thou shalt not support any measure but mine . . . for I thy Lord am a jealous Minister . . .
III	Thou shalt not take the pension of thy Lord the Minister in vain; for I the Minister will force him to accept the Chilterns that taketh my pension in vain.
IV	Remember that thou attend thy Minister's levée day . . .
V	Honour the Regent and the helmets of the Life Guards, that thy stay may be long in the Place, which thy Lord the Minister giveth thee.
VI	Thou shalt not call starving to death murder.
VII	Thou shalt not call Royal gallivanting adultery.
VIII	Thou shalt not say, that to rob the Public is to steal.
IX	Thou shalt bear false witness against the People.
X	Thou shalt not covet the People's applause, thou shalt not covet the People's praise, nor their good name, nor their esteem, nor their reverence, nor any reward that is theirs.

JOHN WILKES' CATECHISM OF A MINISTERIAL MEMBER
by William Hone   1819

The three trials of William Hone are amongst the most remarkable in our constitutional history. They produced more distinct effects upon the temper of the country than any public proceedings of that time. They taught the government a lesson which has never been forgotten, and to which, as much as to any other cause, we owe the prodigious improvement as to the law of libel itself, and to the use of the law, in our own day – an improvement which leaves what is dangerous in the press to be corrected by the remedial power of the press itself; and which, instead of lamenting over the newly-acquired ability of the masses to read seditious and irreligious works, depends upon the general diffusion of this ability as the surest corrective of the evils that are incident even to the best gift of heaven – that of knowledge.

HISTORY OF THE THIRTY YEARS PEACE 1816–1846, vol. I
by Harriet Martineau (first pub. 1858)   Bell, 1877   *p.164*

Crisis and Controversy 1812-1820 3

Between 1812 and 1820, in contrast to the unbroken success of its foreign policy, Liverpool's Government stumbled from one crisis to another at home, and frequently seemed at the point of collapse. Economic distress associated with both wartime and post-war conditions was 'Radicalized' into political agitation after 1815, and the authorities were ill-equipped to deal with either the distress itself or the resultant problems of public order. Without a proper police force, ministers and magistrates had to use troops to keep order and spies to obtain information, and the Government came under bitter attack from both Radicals and Whigs for its handling of the situation.

At the same time, a number of major policy problems placed the Government in further embarrassment: the question of taxation to meet increased expenditure; the argument over agricultural protection; the issue of the currency and the restoration of the Gold Standard; and in 1820, the crisis caused by the return to England of Queen Caroline. All of these aroused great controversy and opposition to the Ministry in the country as well as in Parliament, where many of its supporters temporarily deserted; and by the end of 1820 the Administration was at its lowest ebb.

Was the Government attitude towards demands for relief and reform justifiable?

Canning on Parliamentary Reform, which he feared would be the first step to revolution:

> To that reform indeed he should always be a decided opponent, whatever disguise it assumed, or in whatever form it was presented; whether it exhibited itself in the coarse, broad, gross, disgusting, tyrannical and insulting shape in which of late it had appeared in other places, or in the more plausible and less offensive, but not less dangerous character in which it was occasionally laid before that House.

PARLIAMENTARY DEBATES, *1st Series, vol.40, (1819) col.196*

Liverpool to Grenville, who had sent him a memorandum on the threat of revolution on the French model at the time of the uproar following Peterloo:

> Though it cannot be denied that the great increase of our manufacturing population, the dependence of a great part of that population on foreign demand, and the refinements in machinery (which enable manufacturers to perform that work in weeks, which formerly occupied months, and which lead consequently to extravagant wages at one time, and to low and inadequate ones at another) have recently subjected, and must in the nature of things subject this country to evils with which in the same degree we were formerly unacquainted; yet all these circumstances would not have accounted for the present state of the public mind in certain parts of the country if the events of the French Revolution had not directed the attention of the lower orders of the community, and those immediately above them, to political considerations; had not shaken all respect for established authority and ancient institutions; and had not familiarised mankind with a system of organisation which has been justly represented to be as ingenious and appropriate to its purpose as any invention in mechanics.
>
> THE LIFE OF LORD LIVERPOOL, vol.2
> *by C.D. Yonge   Macmillan, 1868*   *p.431*

The report of the Parliamentary Committee on petitions for relief from the cotton weavers, 1812, shows how *laissez faire* ideas were already accepted as sacred:

> While the Committee fully acknowledge and most deeply lament the great distress of numbers of persons engaged in the cotton manufacture, they are of opinion that no interference of the legislature with the freedom of trade, or with the perfect liberty of every individual to dispose of his time and of his labour in the way and on the terms which he may judge most conducive to his own interest, can take place without violating general principles of the first importance to the prosperity and happiness of the community, without establishing the most pernicious precedent, or without aggravating, after a very short time, the pressure of the general distress, and imposing obstacles against that distress ever being removed.
>
> PARLIAMENTARY DEBATES, *1st Series, vol. 20, (1811) col.609*

Liverpool took a similar view:

> In these cases the Legislature ought not to interfere, but should leave everything to find its own level.... I am satisfied that government or parliament never meddle in these matters at all but they do harm, more or less. ... The evils inseparable from the state of things should not be charged on any government; and, on

enquiry, it would be found that by far the greater part of the miseries of which human nature complained were at all times and in all countries beyond the control of human legislation.

WATERLOO TO PETERLOO
by R.J. White   Penguin, 1968   *p.60*

William Cobbett did not agree:

> Society ought not to exist, if not for the benefit of the whole. It is and must be against the law of nature, if it exists for the benefit of the few and for the misery of the many. I say, then, distinctly, that a society, in which the common labourer ... cannot secure a sufficiency of food and raiment, is a society which ought not to exist; a society contrary to the law of nature; a society whose compact is dissolved.

COBBETT'S POLITICAL REGISTER   *11 September 1819*

Nor, more surprisingly, did the Tory *Quarterly Review*:

> Of distresses, such as now pervade the mass of the community, small indeed is the part which parliaments or governments either create or cure. ... But what little might have been in our power ... has unhappily, perhaps inadvertently, been thrown away. In passing from a state of war to a state of peace, the shock of the revulsion might not improbably have been lessened to all orders of society by somewhat graduating the transition.... If stagnant manufactures, and languishing agriculture, and a population suddenly turned loose from the military or naval services of the country, produce a supply of hands for which there is no work, a partial and temporary remedy might perhaps have been found in undertakings of public utility and magnificence – in the improvement of roads, the completion of canals, the erection of our National Monuments for Waterloo and Trafalgar – undertakings which government might have supplied, if the means had been available.

THE QUARTERLY REVIEW, vol.16   *1816*   *pp.276–277*

Can the Government's handling of the unrest be vindicated?

To answer this question it is necessary to examine the main episodes of unrest, to assess the extent of the threat and the methods used to deal with it in each case.

1.   The Luddites

Report of the Secret Committee on the Disturbed State of Several Counties, 1812:

> It is the opinion of persons, both in civil and military stations, well acquainted with the state of the country, an opinion grounded

upon various information from various quarters now before your committee, but which, for obvious reasons, they do not think proper to detail, that the views of some of the persons engaged in these proceedings have extended to revolutionary measures of the most dangerous description.

Their proceedings manifest a degree of caution and organisation which appears to flow from the direction of some persons under whose influence they act. ...

PARLIAMENTARY DEBATES, *1st Series, vol.23, (1812) col.1036*

General Maitland, in command of 12,000 troops used against the Luddites, to Sidmouth, 10 June 1812:

At present the whole of these Revolutionary Movements are limited to the lowest orders of the people generally, to the places where they show themselves, and no concert exists, nor no plan is laid, further than is manifested in the open acts of violence that are daily committed.

PUBLIC RECORD OFFICE H.O. 40/1

One of the most serious Luddite incidents was the burning of West Houghton mill, Lancashire, in April 1812. The Whig M.P. Samuel Whitbread referred to this in the House of Commons:

As to the persons who had blackened their faces, and disfigured themselves for the purposes of concealment, and had attended the meeting on Deanmoor, near Manchester, it turned out that ten of them were spies sent out by the magistrates. ... These spies were the very ringleaders of the mischief, and incited the people to acts which they would not otherwise have thought of.

PARLIAMENTARY DEBATES, *1st Series, vol. 23, (1812) col.1000*

There is no evidence whatever of any political motives on the part of the Luddites. There is not a single instance in which it can be proved that a Luddite attack was directed towards anything deeper than disputes between masters and men, between workmen and their employers. ... It is suspicious that while machine-breaking was the most prominent feature of the actual disturbances, and while machine breaking, raids for arms, and provision riots were the only overt acts of disorder (apart from common robbery), these aspects of the situation received far less emphasis in the spies' reports than revolutionary plans which never materialised.

POPULAR DISTURBANCES AND PUBLIC ORDER IN REGENCY ENGLAND
by F.O. Darvall (first pub. 1934) O.U.P., 1970 pp.174, 279

2. The Spa Fields Riots, the 'Blanketeers' and the Derbyshire Rising, 1816–1817

Report of the Secret Committee into the Disturbed State of the Country, February 1817:

Attempts have been made, in various parts of the country, as well as in the metropolis, to take advantage of the distress in which the labouring and manufacturing classes of the community are at present involved, to induce them to look for immediate relief, not only in a reform of Parliament on the plan of universal suffrage and annual election, but in a total overthrow of all existing establishments, and in a division of the landed, and extinction of the funded property of the country.

PARLIAMENTARY DEBATES, *1st Series, vol. 35, (1817) col.438*

This refers to men like Thistlewood and the Watsons, who were involved in the Spa Fields Riots, tried for treason and acquitted: they were followers of Thomas Spence, who died in 1814 and had advocated an equal distribution of the land. At their trial the defence counsel, Wetherell, a High Tory, exposed the role of another spy:

If you bear in mind who is the principal (I should say the only) witness in this case – a man of the name of Castle; if you bear in mind what he has proved to have done in the course of these transactions; if you bear in mind for whom he is a witness, from what place he comes, what he has been, and what he now is . . . you will hereafter consider whether Mr. Castle is not the man who has made these persons his dupes; whether he has not alone invented, organised and framed the whole of the projects which he represents were moulded into a system of conspiracy; whether, according to every fair and rational presumption, he is not the author and parent of all these transactions, forming an ideal conspiracy for purposes of his own.

STATE TRIALS, vol. 32   *pp.421–422*

A prosecution witness against the Derbyshire conspirators stated:

On the morning of Tuesday 10th I went on the road towards Eastwood, where I met a considerable body of men armed with pikes; I returned to Nottingham and procured some troops from the barracks ... eighteen privates ... and a subaltern officer. ... When we got as far as Kimberley, a village about four miles from Nottingham and about two miles short of Eastwood, the people told us that the mob, on hearing of the soldiers coming, had dispersed; we followed the route they had taken, and found a quantity of arms, pikes and guns, scattered about on the road.

STATE TRIALS, vol. 32   *p.860*

Another witness referred to a conversation before the Rising with one of its leaders:

I asked him what the poor women and children were to do; he said there would be a provisional government formed and sent down into the country to relieve the wives and children of those that were gone away. ...

Mr. Cross (for the defence): So that you see these hungry paupers wanted a provisional government to supply them with food ... that was their idea of the alteration they proposed of the government.

STATE TRIALS, vol.32   *pp.809, 878*

Lord Fitzwilliam, the Whig Lord-Lieutenant of Yorkshire, wrote to Sidmouth about this episode, blaming the spy 'Oliver' for what had happened:

There certainly prevails very generally in the country a strong and decided opinion that most of the events that have recently occurred in the country are to be attributed to the presence and active agitation of Mr. Oliver. He is considered as the *main spring* from which every movement has taken its rise. All the mischievous in the country have considered themselves as subordinate members of a great leading body of revolutionists in London, as co-operating with that body for one general purpose, and in this view to be under its instructions and directions, communicated by some delegate appointed for the purpose. Had not then a person pretending to come from that body and for that purpose, made his appearance in the country, it is not assuming too much to say that probably no movement whatever would have occurred – it does not follow that a dangerous spirit could not have been found lurking in any breast, but that that spirit would not have found its way into action.

ENGLISH HISTORICAL DOCUMENTS, vol.11 (1783–1832)

edited by A. Aspinall and E.A. Smith   Eyre & Spottiswoode, 1959   p.332

In March 1817 the intended 'March of the Blanketeers' was broken up by troops. A magistrates' spy reported on the assembly of the marchers in Manchester:

Drummond said . . . . We will let them see it is not riot and disturbance we want, it is bread we want and we will apply to our noble Prince as a child would to its Father for bread. If the whole hosts of hell come against me I will not stir an inch; for so must the soldiers or anything else be that come to oppose so lawful and constitutional a proceeding. Whatever you do behave orderly and show your enemies that decorum they themselves ought to show. Baguley said . . . . Now, gentlemen, if any one breaks the peace we will deliver him up to the first magistrate we come to.

LANCASHIRE REFORMERS 1816–1817

by H.W.C. Davis   BULLETIN OF THE JOHN RYLAND LIBRARY, 1926   *pp.76–77*

Drummond and Baguley were reported by other agents as among the most extreme and headstrong of the Manchester Radicals. A month

George Cruikshank's comment on the Government's use of spies such as Castle and Oliver (centre). Castlereagh is seated on the right, facing Canning; Sidmouth is on the left, with Reynolds, an Irish agent. Notice the bag of Radical threats, and the words of John Bull, seen at the window (right).

earlier, another agent reported on a Radical meeting, when the King and the Prince Regent were attacked:

> Mr. Drummond arose and stated, i.e. asked, what business a man had with £39,000 per annum, and another with £38,000, another with two millions who had lost his senses if ever he had any – another man with 1,500,000, our illustrious, gracious, good or rather shall I say big fat man – what right have they with this money – whilst those whom they have robbed are starving for want. A great deal he said of a similar nature. Mr. Baguley attempted to prove from the Magna Charta Act what he had stated on the Monday night before respecting the seizure of the King. He would have gone to great lengths if he had not been called to order by the Chairman. . . .

LANCASHIRE REFORMERS 1816–1817
by H.W.C. Davis   BULLETIN OF THE JOHN RYLAND LIBRARY, 1926   *p.74*

The Government suspended Habeas Corpus and passed the Seditious Meetings Act in February and March 1817. Sidmouth justified these measures in the House of Lords on 24 February 1817:

In many parts of the country, proceedings were still carried on of a most dangerous nature, and which could only come to the knowledge of ministers through the medium of persons who could not be brought into a court of justice.... He required the suspension of the Habeas Corpus Act, in pity to the peaceable and loyal inhabitants of the country; he required it for the protection of the two Houses of Parliament, for the maintenance of our liberties, and for the security of the blessings of the constitution.... To suspend the Habeas Corpus Act at the present moment would be to obstruct the commission of the most flagrant crimes, and check the hands of the sacreligious despoilers of the sacred fabric of the constitution.

PARLIAMENTARY DEBATES, *1st Series, vol.35, (1817) cols. 557–558*

For the Whig opposition, Grey took a different view:

Perhaps, my lords, under so great an accumulation of misery, such exemplary patience, forbearance, resignation and confidence in the existing constitution and government of the country, were never before exhibited.... I think it is a most unfortunate circumstance, a most lamentable necessity, that, at this period of distress and misery, when no measure of relief has been adopted, when no one efficient measure of reduction and retrenchment has been carried into effect ... a measure should be proposed which ... may lead to some invasion or infringement of the people's rights.

PARLIAMENTARY DEBATES, *1st Series, vol.35, (1817) cols. 199–200*

Eight opposition peers entered a protest against the Seditious Meetings Bill:

Dissentient. Because it appears to us that this statute, in inflicting the penalty of death, is unjustly severe; that it gives to magistrates a formidable and unnecessary power, improperly controlling the general expression of opinion, and interfering both with the public and private meetings of the people, in times of which we consider the danger to be much exaggerated, and which we think call for measures of conciliation and relief, and not for coercion.

PARLIAMENTARY DEBATES, *1st Series, vol.35, (1817) col.1270*

Two later views of the conduct of the Government:

A Government that wanted an excuse for suspending the Habeas Corpus Act had found the machinations of their spies a most convenient pretext, and it was obvious that the temptation to use them deliberately as agents provocateurs might be too much for terrified and unprincipled ministers.

THE SKILLED LABOURER 1760–1832

by J.L. and B. Hammond (first pub. 1917)   Longmans, 1932   p.372

The conduct of the Ministry, which in an admirable degree mingled compassion with firmness in the measures which they adopted in dealing with the guilty, contributed greatly to the early restoration not only of tranquillity but of loyalty; for while carrying out the extreme penalties of the law in the case of the ringleaders and exciters of the riots which had taken place, they spared their dupes altogether.

THE LIFE OF LORD LIVERPOOL, vol.2
by C.D. Yonge   Macmillan, 1868   *p.324*

3.   Peterloo, 16 August 1819, and the Six Acts

The very term 'Peterloo Massacre' indicates how this, the most significant event of all, has entered into the mythology of the period. Controversy over what happened began at once, and the contemporary accounts are contradictory.

Was the meeting a threat to public order, justifying its dispersal? Did the authorities deliberately plan to teach the Radical masses a lesson? Is the term 'massacre' appropriate?

Five Lancashire magistrates wrote to Sidmouth on 1 July:

> We cannot have a doubt that some alarming insurrection is in contemplation. . . . [We] cannot but applaud the hitherto peaceful demeanour of many of the labouring classes, yet we do not calculate upon their remaining unmoved. Urged on by the harangues of a few desperate demagogues, we anticipate at no distant period a general rising, and possessing no power to prevent the meetings which are weekly held, we as magistrates are at a loss how to stem the influence of the dangerous and seditious doctrines which are continually disseminated.

PETERLOO: THE CASE REOPENED
by R. Walmsley   M.U.P., 1969   *p.72*

John Tyas, *The Times* correspondent who was at St. Peter's Fields on 16 August, by chance found himself on the hustings with Hunt and was accidentally arrested; he was an unbiased witness of what happened, and his account was the main basis for *The Times* editorial on 19 August:

> It appears by every account that has yet reached London, that in the midst of the Chairman's speech, within *less than twenty minutes* from the commencement of the meeting, the Yeomanry Cavalry of the town of Manchester charged the populace sword in hand, cut their way to the platform, and with the police at their head, made prisoners of HUNT and several of those who surrounded him –

seized the flags of the Reformers – trampled down and cut down a number of the people, who, after throwing some stones and brickbats at the cavalry in its advance towards the hustings, fled on all sides in the utmost confusion and dismay. Of the crowd ... a large portion consisted of women. About 8 or 10 persons were killed, and, besides those whom their own friends carried off, above 50 wounded were taken to the hospitals; but the gross number is not supposed to have fallen short of 80 or 100, more or less, grievously wounded. ...

Was that [meeting] at Manchester an 'unlawful assembly'? Was the notice of it unlawful? We believe not. Was the subject proposed for discussion [a reform in the House of Commons] an unlawful object? Assuredly not. Was any thing done at this meeting before the cavalry rode in upon it, either contrary to law or in breach of the peace? No such circumstance is recorded in any of the statements which have yet reached our hands.

THE TIMES, 19 August 1819

The magistrates reported to Sidmouth on the evening of Peterloo:

There was no appearance of arms or pikes, but great plenty of sticks and staves.... Long before ... [Hunt's arrival] the magistrates had felt a decided conviction that the array was such as to terrify all the King's subjects, and was such as no legitimate purpose could justify .... While the cavalry was forming, a most marked defiance of them was acted by the reforming part of the mob.

PETERLOO: THE CASE REOPENED
by R. Walmsley   M.U.P., 1969   *p.237*

The Government backed up the magistrates, which may suggest collusion in the action. Liverpool to Canning, 23 September 1819:

When I say that the proceedings of the magistrates at Manchester ... were justifiable, you will understand me as not by any means deciding that the course which they pursued on that occasion was in all its parts prudent. A great deal might be said in their favour even on this head; but, whatever judgement might be formed in this respect, being satisfied that they were substantially right, there remained no alternative but to support them.

ENGLISH HISTORICAL DOCUMENTS, vol.11 (1783–1832)
edited by A. Aspinall and E.A. Smith   Eyre & Spottiswoode, 1959   p.334

Canning himself made clear why the Government saw no alternative:

To let down the magistrates would be to invite their resignations and to lose all gratuitous service in the counties liable to disturbance for ever. It is, to be sure, very provoking that the magistrates, right as they were in principle, and nearly right in

A famous cartoon on the Peterloo Massacre. What is its value as historical evidence? Notice the words attributed to the Prince Regent (top left).

practice, should have spoilt the completeness of their case by half an hour's precipitation.
British Museum Add. MSS. 38,741 f.314

A letter from the Home Office to the magistrates in Manchester, before Peterloo:

Reflexion convinces him [Sidmouth] the more strongly of the inexpediency of attempting forcibly to prevent the meeting on Monday. Every discouragement and obstacle should be thrown in its way. ... He has no doubt that you will make arrangements for obtaining evidence of what passes; that if anything illegal is done or said, it may be the subject of prosecution. But even if they should utter sedition ... it will be the wisest course to abstain from any endeavour to disperse the mob, unless they should proceed to acts of felony or riot.
PUBLIC RECORD OFFICE H.O. 41/4, 4 August 1819

One modern historian believes that this has the air of having been written 'for the record':

If any 'Peterloo decision' was reached by Sidmouth and the magistrates it is likely to have been reached privately in the week before the meeting. And it is highly unlikely that any record would have been left in the official Home Office papers for subsequent inspection. ... My opinion is (a) that the Manchester authorities certainly intended to employ force, (b) that Sidmouth knew – and assented to – their intention to arrest Hunt in the midst of the assembly and to disperse the crowd, but that he was unprepared for the violence with which this was effected.... It really was a massacre ... the panic of class hatred.

THE MAKING OF THE ENGLISH WORKING CLASS
by E.P. Thompson   Penguin, 1968   *pp.750, 752*

This verdict may be compared to the view of the leading modern authority on Peterloo:

The repression of the Tory government in 1817 and 1819 is not to be likened to that of Metternich or Alexander I. Peterloo ... was never desired or precipitated by the Liverpool Ministry as a bloody repressive gesture for keeping down the lower orders. If the Manchester magistrates had followed the spirit of Home Office policy there would never have been a 'massacre'.

PETERLOO
by Donald Read   M.U.P., 1958   *p.207*

The Government used the unrest in 1819 as the reason, or excuse, for passing the Six Acts, outlined by Sidmouth in the House of Lords on 30 November 1819:

A conspiracy existed for the subversion of the constitution in church and state, and of the rights of property.... He should now describe the measures designed to meet this evil.... It was proposed, that any person having been tried, convicted and punished for a blasphemous or seditious libel, should on conviction of a second offence, be liable ... to fine, imprisonment, banishment, or transportation ... [and] that all publications, consisting of less than a given number of sheets, should be subjected to a duty equal to that paid by newspapers. ...

To obviate the danger of tumultuous and seditious meetings ... any parties wishing to meet for consideration of subjects connected with church or state, should notify their intention by a requisition signed by seven householders, and it should be illegal for any person not usually inhabiting the place where it was called, to attend. It was proposed to give the magistrates the power, with some limitations, of appointing the time and place of meeting. ...

It was proposed to prohibit military training except under the authority of a magistrate, or lord lieutenant of the county ... and it had been deemed necessary to give magistrates in the disaffected districts, on evidence affording well-grounded suspicion of arms being collected for illegal purposes, the power of seizing them.

THE ANNUAL REGISTER, vol.61 *1819*   *pp.128–129*

A FREE BORN ENGLISHMAN!
THE ADMIRATION of the WORLD !!!
AND THE ENVY of SURROUNDING NATIONS!!!!

A sardonic view of the state of English freedom under the Six Acts of 1819.

Tierney, the Whig leader in the Commons, replied to these proposals:
Nothing but rigour and coercion were to be resorted to. . . . Would
not the new bills rather exasperate than repress? A dead silence in
the country might for a season be produced by soldiers and penal
laws, but nothing could reconcile the people to the loss of their

rights, or compel them to submit quietly to that grievous deprivation. . . . Property never could be exposed to greater danger ultimately than for a popular representation, as this House called itself, to pass nothing but acts of rigour, and omit all attempts at kindness and conciliation. The right of meeting was not only to be taken away, but the broad liberty of the press was to be invaded. . . . Nothing would satisfy the noble lord but an attack upon the very vital principles of the British constitution. . . . The new laws were not such as the public exigency required; the extent, and even the existence of disaffection was not proved; and until it should be so, it was the duty of every honest man to pause.

PARLIAMENTARY DEBATES, *1st Series, vol.41, (1819) cols. 407–412*

4. The Cato Street Conspiracy, 1820

The Attorney-General at the trial of the conspirators:

It was thought by Englishmen, that the assassination of all His Majesty's ministers would be a proper commencement of the revolution which they wished to bring about. . . . Having effected that, they intended to set fire to various parts of this metropolis, to endeavour to obtain possession of the cannon at the artillery ground, and at the stable of the City Light Horse Volunteers, I believe in Grays-inn-lane – to create as much confusion and dismay as they could by these various operations, and then to establish, what in their various expectations they had imagined themselves capable of erecting, a provisional government, the seat of which was to be at the Mansion-house.

STATE TRIALS, vol.33   *col.719*

To this, defence counsel replied:

The possession of London! . . . I should have thought that . . . any man who had seen the march of a single regiment, would have said at once, there is nothing less probable, than that you would have taken possession of any one parish in London – of any one populous street. . . .

I have looked . . . to the list of witnesses for the Crown, I find the name of one Edwards . . . not a prisoner – not taken up upon this charge – not tainted as an accomplice by government – no treason that we have known of against him – a man cognizant of all the facts – a man present at all the conversations – a man who pointed out the New-Times newspaper [the paper in which the false notice of a cabinet dinner appeared], and saw and knew and guided everything, and yet that man is not called – the spy is not called because the contrivance would have been made evident by his cross-examination. . . . If all the circumstances could be investigated, it would prove that the treasonable part is altogether the brewing of a spy and an informer, to implicate in a charge of high treason, a man who had gone far enough towards losing his own life, but not to the length of that greatest of crimes.

STATE TRIALS, VOL.33   *cols. 864, 889*

In all of these disturbances, it should be asked how serious was the threat to the existing order, and how far the Government can be blamed for instigating trouble through its own agents.

Shelley had no doubt about the role of spies:

It is impossible to know how far the higher members of the Government are involved in the guilt of their infernal agents. . . . But this much is known, that so soon as the whole nation lifted up its voice for parliamentary reform, spies went forth. These were selected from the most worthless and infamous of mankind, and dispersed among the multitude of famished and illiterate labourers. It was their business, if they found no discontent, to create it. It was their business to find victims, no matter whether right or wrong.

From An Address to the People on the Death of the Princess Charlotte
quoted in THE PROSE WORKS OF P.B. SHELLEY, vol.2
edited by H.B. Forman   Reeves & Turner, 1880   *p.110*

This is a view which has been endorsed by historians of the left such as the Hammonds and E.P. Thompson, though sometimes with reservations. Compare the Hammonds' accusation on page 40 with the following on the most notorious case, that of Oliver:

There is no reason to suppose that Sidmouth deliberately employed Oliver for the diabolical purpose of fomenting an abortive rebellion.

THE SKILLED LABOURER 1760–1832
by J.L. and B. Hammond (first pub. 1917)   Longmans, 1932   *p.374*

Sidmouth himself wrote in reply to the charge that Oliver had caused the Derbyshire Rising:

The statement is to me incredible but I think it so important as to require immediate and minute investigation. It is directly at variance with the instructions given to Oliver and with his communications to Sir John Byng [Military commander in the North], as well as to myself. . . . It would have been entirely inconsistent with the instructions given him by Government if he had in any instance fomented or encouraged the disaffected to proceed with greater activity or to greater lengths than they were themselves inclined to do.

ADDINGTON   *by Philip Ziegler   Collins, 1965*   *p.364*

A MAY DAY GARLAND for 1820.

Ministers dance round a maypole bearing the heads of the Cato Street conspirators executed on 1 May 1820. Vansittart, Canning, Sidmouth and Chief Justice Abbott are to the left and Castlereagh and Attorney-General Gifford to the right. Notice Edwards, the government agent, in the background.

General Maitland, dealing with the Luddite disturbances, saw the problem of using spies:

> Those who are willing to undertake mixing with the disaffected are generally of a character whose information must be received with extreme caution, and certainly in the instance of those on whom we could rely, they very much to their credit feel extreme difficulty in going to the lengths they must necessarily do to be of any real utility.

PUBLIC RECORD OFFICE H.O. 42/125, 18 July 1812

The Whig M.P. Brougham put a balanced point of view in the House of Commons over the Cato Street Conspiracy in 1820:

> As long as such men as Thistlewood and the others existed, government were, in his opinion, not only justified in employing persons to watch their proceedings, but would be highly culpable if they did not do so. ... There was, however, one limitation to this doctrine. He who employed spies took upon himself a most difficult and responsible office. He was deeply answerable to the

country and to the administration of justice, if he did not take the greatest care to select such men as would only give information, and not instigate to the commission of crime.

PARLIAMENTARY DEBATES, *2nd Series, vol.1, (1820) col.61*

Why was the Corn Law of 1815 passed, and how successful was it?

Lord Binning spoke for the landowners and farmers:

In the depressed state of agriculture for the last twelve months, some relief was absolutely necessary. Numbers of persons had been turned out of employment, and the pressure of the poor rates was become intolerable.... Most enormous losses had been suffered in the last year; and if some speedy remedy was not administered by the wisdom and firmness of the legislature, the agricultural interest of the country might soon be completely ruined.

PARLIAMENTARY DEBATES, *1st Series, vol.29, (1815) col. 984*

Another M.P. was sure of the cause:

Nothing could be more obvious than that the reduction of the price of corn was attributable to the importation of foreign grain.

PARLIAMENTARY DEBATES, *1st Series, vol.29, (1815) col.1222*

Samuel Whitbread, a Radical Whig and member of the brewing family, supported them:

The proposition was not that rents were too high, but that corn was too low, and that it ought to be raised to such a price as to enable the farmer to cultivate his land with advantage, without reducing the landlord to the necessity of lowering his rents.

PARLIAMENTARY DEBATES, *1st Series, vol.29, (1815) col.1240*

F.J. Robinson spoke as a member of the Government:

He was of the opinion, on the whole, not only that our security would be greater, but even that the price of corn might in the end be cheaper, by home cultivation, than by depending on foreign countries.

PARLIAMENTARY DEBATES, *1st Series, vol.29, (1815) col.802*

G. Philips argued the opposite case in terms anticipating the Anti-Corn Law League:

The committee are invited to adopt measures intended expressly to raise the price of corn, and in his judgement to raise it permanently.... If you raise the price of provisions without proportionably raising that of labour, to what privations and evils must you necessarily expose the labourer! ... The labourer must go to the parish, or turn to some more profitable employment, if by chance any can be found, or he must emigrate, or work himself out by overstrained exertion. ...

If we artificially raise the price of provisions, we shall raise the price of labour, and in the same proportion we shall assist our rivals against ourselves. Is it possible to suppose, that the richest nation in the world ... is to be starved, if it does not provide a sufficiency of corn for its subsistence; because, forsooth, other nations, wanting its commodities, and having more corn than they can consume, will refuse to relieve its deficiency out of their own superfluity? ... An importation of corn cannot take place without a corresponding export of commodities on which British industry has been employed. That export will increase your natural wealth, that wealth will increase your population, and that increased population will provide an increased demand for your agricultural produce.

PARLIAMENTARY DEBATES, *1st Series, vol.29, (1815) cols. 811–817*

Cobbett took a practical farmer's attitude:

I deny that it is in the *power* of even a *body* of men, who have been called *omnipotent*, to cause the farmer to have a high price; the price depending on the *crop*, and not upon any law or any regulation. ... I am no advocate for *law* that is now pending. I know, that the thing will, and must, regulate itself.

COBBETT'S POLITICAL REGISTER, 21 May 1814

The Annual Register, after describing the popular riots against the Corn Law, dealt with its results:

The consequences of this measure were by no means such as were expected either by its promoters or opposers. The effects either of former importations, or, more probably, of two plentiful harvests, and a greatly extended culture of grain, were to produce a gradual steady reduction of price, so that, instead of approaching the limits fixed for importation, it sunk to a level below that of several years past. The farmers, who were labouring under exorbitant rents, in addition to other increased expenses, were general sufferers; and the landlords found it necessary in many instances to make great abatements in their dues. In the result, many leases have been voided, and farms have been left without tenants.

THE ANNUAL REGISTER, vol.57 *1815*   *p.6*

Huskisson explained how the Government came to adopt the provisions of the Act:

I have always considered a graduated duty as a much wiser and more efficacious regulation than a contingent prohibition ... but at a very full meeting of the landed interest at Fife House [Lord Liverpool's London house], when the option was in their power,

The Blessings of Peace or the Curse of the Corn Bill

A bitter comment by Cruikshank on the Corn Law of 1815. Rich landlords refuse to allow cheap foreign corn into the country, while John Bull and his family emigrate. How fair a view is this?

the Gentlemen present almost unanimously, and particularly Mr. Western [the main spokesman for the landed interest], gave a preference to the present Bill.
British Museum Add. MSS. 38,742 f.4

Part of the Declaration of a Radical meeting in Manchester in January 1819:

The conduct of the late Parliament in passing the Corn Bill, which was obtained under false pretensions and passed at the point of the bayonet, in defiance of the united groans and supplications of the People, was oppressive in its design and cruel in its operation; being neither more nor less than a vile conspiracy between the great Landholders and the Ministers, to extort from the industrious labourer and mechanic, through the very bread they eat, an immense portion of Taxes for the support of the Borough system, and to enrich themselves and their pensioned minions, by the sweat of the poor man's brow.

PETERLOO
by Donald Read   M.U.P., 1958   *p.212*

Amending the 1815 Law in 1828, Huskisson looked back over its operation:

> He lamented, from the bottom of his soul, the mass of evil and miseries and destruction of capital which that law, in the course of its twelve years' operation, had produced. And he did believe that ... the effect of the bill, as far as regarded the agriculturists themselves, had been to keep the prices of produce lower, for those twelve years, than they would have been, even if the corn trade had been entirely open.

THE CORN LAWS AND SOCIAL ENGLAND
by C.R. Fay   C.U.P., 1932   *pp.79–80*

Wheat Prices (shillings per quarter) in five-year averages, with Rousseaux price indices. (100 = average of 1865 and 1885)

	Wheat	Overall Index
1790–4	49.57	–
1800–4	84.85	167
1810–4	102.45	194
1815–9	80.35	155
1820–4	57.15	122
1825–9	62.47	118

ABSTRACT OF BRITISH HISTORICAL STATISTICS
by B.R. Mitchell and P. Deane   C.U.P., 1962   pp.486–489, 471–473

How successful was the Government's handling of finance?

Revenue for 1815

	£	
Customs	10,487,522	
Excise	26,562,432	
Income Tax	14,318,572	These figures are not en-
Assessed Taxes	6,214,987	tirely accurate, but give an
Stamps & Post		idea of the relative impor-
Office	7,413,413	tance of the different sou-
Land Taxes	1,079,993	rces of revenue.
Other sources	366,883	
Total	66,443,802	

PARLIAMENTARY DEBATES, *1st Series, vol.32, (1816) cols.431–432*

In 1816 the Government decided to retain the Income (or Property) Tax temporarily, even though it had been introduced as a wartime emergency tax. Vansittart put the Government's case in the House of Commons:

Economical Humbug of 1816 or: saving at the Spiggot & letting out at the Bunghole

This attack on government spending shows taxes pouring into the vat, while Vansittart, the Chancellor of the Exchequer, allows only a trickle of money for the Public Service, to John Bull's dismay. Meanwhile, the Prince Regent has removed a large bung, and he and his friends collect a flood of money, while Liverpool and Castlereagh (left) carry barrels on their heads for Household Troops and the Standing Army and for Sinecures, Pensions and Places.

This tax would press less on the lower orders of society than any tax which could be devised. ... It was a tax more upon the rich than upon the poor.... When the act was revised, it would be found the least oppressive and the least objectionable of any tax that had ever been imposed.... A small portion of the property tax would be less burthensome than those taxes on consumption, which, though less immediately felt, were ultimately more burthensome and less productive.... No minister had pledged himself to its indispensable continuance ... it was continued only for the purpose of defraying the extraordinary charges occasioned by the war in the first years of peace.

PARLIAMENTARY DEBATES, *1st Series, vol.33, (1816) cols.240, 425–433*

Petition from the Corporation of London against the Property Tax:
The petitioners have learnt with the most serious alarm, that it is

54

George Cruikshank's earthy comment on the Ministry's discomfiture caused by the rejection of Income Tax. From the left, Castlereagh, Ellenborough, Eldon, the Prince Regent, McMahon (the Prince's secretary), Vansittart.

the intention of His Majesty's ministers, in violation of their assurances, and the solemn faith of parliament, to propose to the House the continuance or modification of the tax upon income, commonly called the property-tax. . . . Painful experience has only served the more strongly to root upon their minds a conviction of its injustice, vexation and oppression . . . the manner in which the said tax is carried into execution, by means of an odious, arbitrary and detestable inquisition into the most private concerns and circumstances of individuals, is still more vexatious, unjust and oppressive, hostile to every sense of freedom, revolting to the feelings of Englishmen, and repugnant to the principles of the British Constitution; . . . the petitioners are deeply sensible of the depressed state of the agricultural interests, and of the ruinous effect of such a burden thereon; . . . the manufacturing and trading interests are equally depressed, and equally borne down with the weight of taxation . . . and they confidently hoped, that by such reductions in the public expenditure, . . . and the abolishing of all unnecessary places, pensions and sinecures, there would have been no pretence for the continuation of a tax subversive of freedom, and destructive of the peace and happiness of the people.

PARLIAMENTARY DEBATES, *1st Series, vol.32, (1816) cols.433–434*

Castlereagh to the Prince Regent, 18 March 1816:

Lord Castlereagh has with much regret to inform your Royal Highness that the Property Tax has been rejected by the House of Commons by 238 to 201 – majority 37. The calculation of the Treasury this morning was that we should carry it by 40, but this was defeated by numbers of the friends of the Government going away and some going against, whose support had been calculated upon. ... This defalcation leaves us with but 12 millions of clear revenue to meet this year's expenditure of 30 millions, and taking the future peace establishment at 20 millions a year, there will exist a serious deficiency of means to meet the charge.

THE LETTERS OF GEORGE IV 1812–1830, vol. 2
edited by A. Aspinall   C.U.P., 1938   *p.160*

Apart from the burden of taxation, the other major financial controversy was over the restoration of the Gold Standard, suspended as a war emergency measure in 1797, when the Government released the Bank of England from the obligation of paying cash for its notes.

The 'Bullion Report' of 1811 on the wartime inflation:

There is at present an excess in the paper circulation of this country, of which the most unequivocal symptom is the very high price of bullion, and next to that, the low state of the continental exchanges; this excess is to be ascribed to the want of sufficient check and control in the issues of paper from the Bank of England; and originally, to the suspension of cash payments, which removed the natural and true control. ... Your Committee therefore ... report it ... as their opinion that the system of the circulating medium of this country ought to be brought back, with as much speed as is compatible with a wise and necessary caution, to the original principle of cash payments at the option of the holder of Bank paper.

ENGLISH HISTORICAL DOCUMENTS, vol.11 (1783–1832)
edited by A. Aspinall and E.A. Smith   Eyre & Spottiswoode, 1959
pp.593–594

Peel announced the Government's decision to restore cash payments in 1819:

In consequence of the evidence and the discussions upon it, his opinion with regard to this question had undergone a material change. ... He had called upon the House to affirm the necessity for the adoption of a metallic standard. ... Every sound writer on the subject came to the same conclusion, that a certain weight of

THE

BANK RESTRICTION BAROMETER;

OR, SCALF OF EFFECTS ON SOCIETY OF THE

Bank Note System, and Payments in Gold.

BY ABRAHAM FRANKLIN.

*** *To be read from the words* " BANK RESTRICTION," *in the middle,*
upwards or downwards.

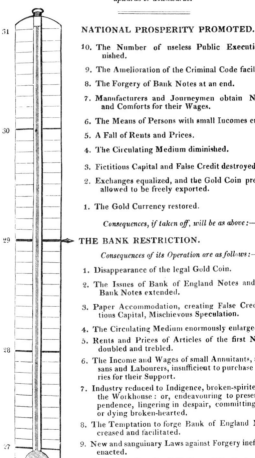

NATIONAL PROSPERITY PROMOTED.

10. The Number of useless Public Executions diminished.

9. The Amelioration of the Criminal Code facilitated.

8. The Forgery of Bank Notes at an end.

7. Manufacturers and Journeymen obtain Necessaries and Comforts for their Wages.

6. The Means of Persons with small Incomes enlarged.

5. A Fall of Rents and Prices.

4. The Circulating Medium diminished.

3. Fictitious Capital and False Credit destroyed.

2. Exchanges equalized, and the Gold Coin preserved, if allowed to be freely exported.

1. The Gold Currency restored.

Consequences, if taken off, will be as above:—viz.

THE BANK RESTRICTION.

Consequences of its Operation are as follows:—viz.

1. Disappearance of the legal Gold Coin.

2. The Issues of Bank of England Notes and Country Bank Notes extended.

3. Paper Accommodation, creating False Credit, Fictitious Capital, Mischievous Speculation.

4. The Circulating Medium enormously enlarged.

5. Rents and Prices of Articles of the first Necessity, doubled and trebled.

6. The Income and Wages of small Annuitants, and Artisans and Labourers, insufficient to purchase Necessaries for their Support.

7. Industry reduced to Indigence, broken-spirited, and in the Workhouse : or, endeavouring to preserve independence, lingering in despair, committing suicide, or dying broken-hearted.

8. The Temptation to forge Bank of England Notes increased and facilitated.

9. New and sanguinary Laws against Forgery ineffectually enacted.

10. Frequent and useless inflictions of the barbarous Punishment of Death.

GENERAL DISTRESS INCREASED.

From a leaflet of 1819 supporting the restoration of the Gold Standard
and the end of Bank Restriction, that is, the suspension since 1797 of
the Bank of England's obligation to pay out gold coin in exchange for
its notes.

gold bullion, with an impression on it, denoting it to be of that certain weight, and of a certain fineness, constituted the only true, intelligible and adequate standard of value. ... It was idle, while such distress existed, to speak of national prosperity.... That the excess of commercial speculation, which led to such evils, was the consequence of an over issue of paper currency, was a fact not to be disputed. A check upon that issue was the only cure that could be applied, and it must be applied by the establishment of a metallic standard of value.

PARLIAMENTARY DEBATES, *1st Series, vol.40, (1819) cols.677–683*

Petition of between four and five hundred merchants of London, 1819:

Your petitioners have reason to apprehend, that measures are in contemplation with reference to the resumption of cash payments by the Bank of England which in the opinion of your petitioners will ... tend to a forced, precipitate and highly injurious contraction of the circulating medium of the country.

The consequences of such contraction will, as your petitioners humbly conceive, be to add to the burthen of the public debt; greatly to increase the pressure of the taxes; to lower the value of all landed and commercial property; seriously to affect both public and private credit; to embarrass and reduce all the operations of agriculture, manufactures and commerce, and to throw out of employment (as in the calamitous year of 1816) a great proportion of the industrious and labouring classes of the community.

PARLIAMENTARY DEBATES, *1st Series, vol.40, (1819) col.599*

The operation of the Gold Standard was strongly attacked on the above grounds during the economic crisis of 1822, and defended by Huskisson:

The proposition was made for a depreciation of the standard of the currency.... How strange must be the condition of this country, if it can only prosper by a violation of national faith and a subversion of private property – if it can only be saved by a measure, reprobated by all statesmen and all historians – the wretched but antiquated resource of barbarian ignorance and arbitrary power, and only known among civilised countries, as the last mark of a nation's weakness and degradation.... If you once lower your standard it will become a precedent that will be resorted to on every future emergency or temporary pressure.... When men find that, in England, there is no security in pecuniary contracts, they will seek that security elsewhere. If we once embark in this career ... England, depend upon it, will rapidly descend, and not more rapidly in character than in wealth, to the level of those countries, in which, from ignorance or barbarism, such expedients are not yet exploded.

Why did the case of Queen Caroline in 1820 present a threat to the Government?

> Political party spirit made the presence of the queen acceptable to many, who cared nothing about her, except so far as she was a means of annoyance to ministers, and who, even in former times when she was protected by the late king, had been connected with her adversaries. The radicals naturally became her partisans; because they had no better means of decrying the king, than by the eager defence of her cause.
>
> THE ANNUAL REGISTER, vol.62   *1820*   *pp.140–141*

Stuart Wortley, M.P., accused the Whigs of exploiting the issue for party purposes, with reference to their motion to restore the Queen's name to the liturgy, 31 January 1821:

> It was impossible to deny that those who had voted for it had wished to use it as a means for turning out the present ministers and putting others into their places.
>
> PARLIAMENTARY DEBATES, *2nd Series, vol.4, (1821) col.225*

The Government found itself trapped between the public's support for Queen Caroline and the King's demand for a divorce.

Stuart Wortley to Liverpool, 18 December 1820:

> The minds of a very great proportion of the better sort of people revolt at anything like harshness to the Queen, because they think that it arises from the King's personal feelings towards her, and that his conduct to her from the beginning has left him no right whatever to complain of any part of hers. This is the real cause of the failure of the bill in the House of Lords, and would have made it absolutely impossible to pass it in the House of Commons, where public feeling has, of course, so much more weight.
>
> THE LIFE OF LORD LIVERPOOL, vol.3
> *by C.D. Yonge   Macmillan, 1868*   *p.115*

Croker noted the effect of this affair on the relations between King and ministers:

> The King wants the Ministers to pledge themselves to a divorce, which they will not do.... He is furious, and says they have deceived him. ... The King has certainly intimated intentions of looking for new and more useful servants.
>
> CORRESPONDENCE AND DIARIES OF JOHN WILSON CROKER, vol.1
> *edited by L.J. Jennings   Murray, 1884*   *pp.160–161*

The RADICAL LADDER

London Pub.^d by G. Humphrey 27 St James St April 15 1821

*George Cruikshank's view of the affair of Queen Caroline in 1820.
Caroline reaches for the crown, supported by Radicals and Jacobins
whose real object is the destruction of the Constitution. Notice the
weapons, the cap of liberty with the flag of democracy, and the writing on
the ladder – Revolution, Anarchy, Ruin, Cato Street etc. Were the
Radicals really like this?*

4 Liberal Toryism and the Disintegration of the Tories

In the early 1820s a partial reconstruction of the Ministry took place, under the leadership of Liverpool, in which some of the more reactionary members gave way to men who took a more pragmatic view of reform; the accident of Castlereagh's suicide in August 1822 was the catalyst of this process, but other factors were at work too. This chapter examines the motives for these changes, and then goes on to consider how 'liberal' were the subsequent measures of the 'liberal Tories' and how much credit the ministers deserve for them. The rapid disintegration of the Tories after Liverpool's retirement due to a stroke in 1827 led to their loss of office in 1830; the controversy over the reforms, above all over Catholic Emancipation, needs to be analysed in relation to the break-up of the Tory alliance forged by Liverpool in order to explain the decline and fall of the Tories.

What were the reasons for the reconstruction of the Ministry between 1821 and 1823?

Peel to Croker, 23 February 1820:

> Do you not think that the tone of England – of that great compound of folly, weakness, prejudice, wrong feeling, right feeling, obstinacy, and newspaper paragraphs, which is called public opinion – is more liberal – to use an odious but intelligible phrase – than the policy of the government? Do you not think there is a feeling, becoming daily more general and more confirmed – that is, independent of the pressure of taxation, or any immediate cause – in favour of some undefined change in the mode of governing the country? It seems to me a curious crisis – when public opinion never had such influence on public measures, and yet never was so dissatisfied with the share which it possessed.
>
> CORRESPONDENCE AND DIARIES OF JOHN WILSON CROKER, vol. 1
> *edited by L.J. Jennings   Murray, 1884*   *p.170*

Peel's return to the Government in December 1821 as Home Secretary instead of Sidmouth was the first significant change, but this appointment was far from inevitable, as Croker's diary earlier in 1821 indicates: Peel really wanted the Exchequer.

I am sure that, what between his fear of having Peel as his Chancellor of the Exchequer and his desire to force Canning on the King, [Liverpool] would be glad of a general refusal [of office] from Peel, who would have been but too ready to give one if he had not suspected that Lord Liverpool wished for one, which piques him a little.

CORRESPONDENCE AND DIARIES OF JOHN WILSON CROKER, VOL. I

edited by L.J. Jennings   Murray, 1884   *p.190*

In July 1821 Wellington saw the need for the Government to be strengthened:

Mr. Canning's conduct was not very advantageous to us. But viewing the state of the Government, we were convinced that he was the person most likely from his parliamentary talents to assist the Government *if in office*, and on the other hand to be elevated to a station in which he would have the power of being most mischievous if *left out*. ... H.M. refused to act upon our advice. ... If we had not his permission to gain the strength which is within our reach, we must sooner or later be broken down. ... No other party could continue a Government for six months without dissolving the Parliament, and if Parliament should be dissolved by the Whigs, a Radical House of Commons would be the inevitable consequence.

ENGLISH HISTORICAL DOCUMENTS, vol. 11 (1783–1832)

edited by A. Aspinall and E.A. Smith   Eyre & Spottiswoode, 1959
pp.150–151

Historians have disagreed about the degree of 'liberalization' involved in the Cabinet changes of 1821–1822.

The infusion of such new blood strengthened and liberalised Liverpool's ministry. It is noteworthy that nearly half of the Cabinet members now sat in the House of Commons, while in 1815 more than three-fourths had been peers. The Government had become more representative of the middle and mercantile classes, and from them came the impulse for reform. The reaction against reform which characterised Eldonian Conservatism began to break, and although the Chancellor remained on the Woolsack until 1827, he was unable to maintain his hitherto dominant influence. With the entrance of the Canningites to the Liverpool ministry the first real chapter of English reform in the nineteenth century opened. Peel in the Home Office, Huskisson in the Board of Trade, Robinson under Huskisson's guidance at the Exchequer, struck out boldly on new paths and carried measures that entitle the ministry to rank amongst the great reforming administrations of the century.

WILLIAM HUSKISSON AND LIBERAL REFORM

by A. Brady   O.U.P., 1928   *pp.10–11*

E

It is easy to exaggerate the significance of the Cabinet reconstruction of 1821–23. The substitution of Peel for Sidmouth as
Home Secretary was unquestionably a change for the better, but
... we have long since abandoned the view that the substitution of
Canning for Castlereagh produced a marked change in British
foreign policy.... On questions of domestic policy there was little
to choose between them.... Too much, in fact, has sometimes
been made of the distinction between the pre-1822 Tories, and the
progressive Tories under Canning who in that year came to the
fore. That distinction was often blurred.

HENRY HOBHOUSE'S DIARY

edited by A. Aspinall   Home & van Thal, 1947   Introduction, pp.ix–x

How 'liberal' were the 'liberal Tories'?

The King to Lord Liverpool, 27 January 1825:
Can the present Government suppose that the King will permit
any individuals now to force upon him, measures of which he
entirely disapproves; more especially when many members of the
King's present Cabinet hold the same opinions with the King
himself respecting the new political liberalism.

No such thing – if the present line of policy is to be *further*
pursued, the King will feel himself justified in taking such
measures as the Government will be the least prepared to expect.

THE LETTERS OF GEORGE IV 1812–1830, vol.3

edited by A. Aspinall   C.U.P., 1938   *p.99*

Palmerston (Secretary at War in the Government) to William Temple,
17 July 1826:
The Government are as strong as any government can wish to be,
as far as regards those who sit facing them; but in truth the real
opposition of the present day sit behind the Treasury Bench; and it
is by the stupid old Tory party, who bawl out the memory and
praises of Pitt while they are opposing all the measures and
principles which he held most important; it is by these that the
progress of the Government in every improvement which they are
attempting is thwarted and impeded. On the Catholic question; on
the principles of commerce; on the corn laws; on the settlement of
the currency; on the laws regulating the trade in money; on
colonial slavery; on the game laws, which are intimately connected
with the moral habits of the people: on all these questions, and
everything like them, the Government find support from the
Whigs and resistance from their self-denominated friends.

THE LIFE OF PALMERSTON, vol.1

by H.L. Bulwer   Bentley, 1870   *pp.171–172*

Palmerston was a Canningite. Mrs. Arbuthnot saw things in a High Tory light, writing on 28 November 1826:

> The Government, as it is now constituted, has, I think, totally lost (and I own I think justly) the confidence of the country. The liberal party, with Mr. Canning at their head, court the Opposition and try to shape their measures with a view of catching their votes; in order to do this, they discuss measures in the Cabinet as little as they possibly can, not to be thwarted by their illiberal colleagues, and all this naturally incenses the Tory Party to the greatest possible degree.

MRS ARBUTHNOT'S DIARY, vol.2

edited by Francis Bamford and the Duke of Wellington   Macmillan, 1950
pp.59–60

In the same year Tierney, for the Whigs, went even further, in reply to an attack by Canning:

> We are certainly, to all intents and purposes, a branch of his majesty's government. Its proceedings for some time past have proved, that though the gentlemen opposite are in office, we are in power, the measures are ours, but all the emoluments are theirs. ... I think that government do want support. I never saw a session when they wanted it more. ... he [Canning] would, without our support, have been long ago driven from his present honours. If we take away our support out he must go tomorrow.

THE WHIGS IN OPPOSITION

by A. Mitchell   O.U.P., 1967   *p.190*

The Economic Reforms of Huskisson and Robinson

In 1820 Thomas Tooke, a London merchant, presented a Petition which called for free trade, and continued:

> Unfortunately, a policy the very reverse of this has been, and is, more or less adopted and acted upon by the government of this and of every other country, each trying to exclude the productions of other countries, with the specious and well-meant design of encouraging its own productions. ... Of the numerous protective and prohibitory duties of our commercial code, ... while all operate as a very heavy tax on the community at large, very few are of any ultimate benefit to the classes in whose favour they were originally instituted. ... The distress which now so generally prevails is considerably aggravated by that system. ... Nothing would more tend to counteract the commercial hostility of foreign states than the adoption of a more enlightened and more conciliatory policy on the part of this country.

A HISTORY OF PRICES, vol.6

by T. Tooke and W. Newmarch (first pub. 1857)   King & Son, 1928,
pp.333–334

Tooke wrote later that he found some ministers to share his enthusiasm for the ideas of Adam Smith.

> Whatever effect or success might attend the Merchants' Petition of 1820, was due principally to the favour with which its doctrines were regarded by Lord Liverpool and a portion of his Cabinet. There was nothing connected with the preparation or presentation of the Petition which could be construed into pressure on the Government; and the simple truth is, that the Government were, at that time, far more sincere, and resolute Free Traders than the Merchants of London.
>
> A HISTORY OF PRICES, vol.6
> *by T. Tooke and W. Newmarch (first pub. 1857)   King & Son, 1928*
> *p.342*

Liverpool expressed cordial concurrence with the Petition; but in Parliament he drew attention to the practical difficulties:

> If we look to the general principle of freedom of trade, let us, at the same time, look to the state of our laws as they regard agricultural produce. ... Under the operation of these laws, we cannot go to foreign countries on the principle of reciprocal advantage. We will not receive their corn or cattle. With the exception of wine, and some other articles, we will not take what they most wish to give us. ... We have risen to our present greatness under a different system than that of free and unrestricted trade. Some suppose that we have risen in consequence of that system. Others, of whom I am one, believe that we have risen in spite of that system. It is utterly impossible, with our debt and taxation, even if they were but half their existing amount, that we can suddenly adopt the system of free trade.
>
> A HISTORY OF PRICES, vol.6
> *by T. Tooke and W. Newmarch (first pub. 1857)   King & Son, 1928*
> *pp.404-405*

Huskisson justified his tariff cuts in 1825:

> If the article be not manufactured much cheaper or much better abroad than at home, such a duty [30%] is ample for protection. If it be manufactured so much cheaper, or so much better abroad, as to render 30% insufficient, my answer is, first, that a greater protection is only a premium to the smuggler; and secondly, that there is no wisdom in attempting to bolster up a competition, which this degree of protection will not sustain. Let the state have the tax, which is now the reward of the smuggler, and let the consumer have the better and cheaper article, without the painful consciousness that he is consulting his own convenience at the expense of daily violating the laws of his country.
>
> WILLIAM HUSKISSON AND LIBERAL REFORM
> *by A. Brady   O.U.P., 1928*   *p.116*

A modern estimate of Huskisson's work:

The limited nature of Huskisson's tariff reform is apparent. He accepted as wholeheartedly as Peel did later the free trade doctrine, but in its application he was hampered by a number of factors, the most pronounced of which were his party affiliations. He and his associates had to educate both their own party and Parliament. An attempt to effect sweeping changes would merely have stiffened the resistance of the opposition, and perhaps have postponed reform indefinitely. Furthermore, Huskisson believed that in economic policy gradual change was far the soundest.... Hence he defended moderate protection. In addition he wished to test European competition. Whenever he discovered that British industries had little to fear from continental rivals he would reduce further the duties on the foreign articles.... Indeed Huskisson might be accused of slowness in lowering the dykes, when there was little danger from the rising flood.... In full justice ... it should be said that his chief aim was the removal of prohibitions and prohibitive duties, not the abolition of protection, and in respect to the major industries of Britain his new tariff schedules succeeded. Yet the removal of prohibitions was perhaps inadequate. Under the circumstances, further tariff pruning might have benefited the home producer and consumer, and would certainly have increased the revenue.

WILLIAM HUSKISSON AND LIBERAL REFORM
by A. Brady O.U.P., 1928 *pp.119–120*

Huskisson had to steer a course between Radical demands and diehard opposition. Joseph Hume on the 1825 tariff cuts:

As to the general commercial principles upon which the right hon. gentleman had acted, he gave him the fullest credit for their utility and liberality, and only wished him to carry them further.

PARLIAMENTARY DEBATES, *2nd Series, vol.12, (1825) col.746*

The view of the extreme Tories:

Herries [Secretary to the Treasury] told me that Huskisson's indecent presumption and haste in altering the trading laws was creating great alarm and dissatisfaction among the merchants of the City.... Rothschild had been with Mr. Herries and had told him that the consequence of admitting foreign goods (which had not been met by corresponding liberality on the other side of the water) was, that all the gold was going out of the country.

MRS ARBUTHNOT'S DIARY, vol.I
edited by Francis Bamford and the Duke of Wellington Macmillan, 1950
p.391

The extent of progress towards free trade was shown in the Report of the Committee on Import Duties in 1840:

The Tariff of the United Kingdom presents neither congruity nor unity of purpose: ... no fewer than 1150 different rates of duty [are] chargeable on imported articles. ... The duties are sometimes meant to be both productive of revenue, and for protective objects – ends which are frequently inconsistent with each other. ... In the year 1839, out of a total customs revenue of £22,962,000, there were 17 articles which produced 94% of that revenue; and 29 other articles which produced 4% more, – making 98% of the customs revenue from 46 articles.

A HISTORY OF PRICES, vol.6
by T. Tooke and W. Newmarch (first pub. 1857)   King & Son, 1928
pp.423–424

The Repeal of the Anti-Combination Laws

Though Francis Place may have exaggerated his own role in paving the way for the repeal, he gave a good account of how it was managed in Parliament by Joseph Hume.

I was quite certain that if the bills came under discussion in the House they would be lost. Mr. Hume had the good sense to see this, and wholly to refrain from speaking on them. ... No inquiry was made as to who drew the bills; they were found to contain all that was needful, and with some assiduity in seeing members to induce them not to speak on the several readings, they passed the House of Commons almost without the notice of members within or newspapers without.

THE LIFE OF FRANCIS PLACE
by G. Wallas   Allen & Unwin, 1918   *pp.214, 216*

Place was less fair in describing the Government's decision to re-examine the law on trade unions after a wave of strikes, with some violence, had followed the repeal.

Mr. Huskisson commenced his speech by declaring that repealing the Combination Laws seemed likely to be attended with the most inconvenient and dangerous consequences.... He complained that the Committee had made no report, and he made several objections to the resolutions. He excused himself for neither having attended in his place in the Committee, nor to the progress of the bill in Parliament, and having thus cleared his way, he fell furiously to work upon his subject. He pulled the Act to pieces; complained of it as an anomaly. It not only repealed the statute law, but forbade the operation of the common law, which had thus introduced a great public evil.... The bill had been hurried through the House without discussion. He then drew a false and exaggerated picture of the state of the country, and predicted the most fatal consequences. Liberty, property, life itself was in danger, and Parliament must speedily interfere.

THE LIFE OF FRANCIS PLACE
by G. Wallas   Allen & Unwin, 1918   *pp.224–225*

The Government introduced its own Combination Bill in 1825, on which Liverpool spoke.

> The measure arose almost entirely out of the bill of last session, which had been hastily passed. He had not been aware of its extent, and did not, until it came into operation, know its provisions. . . . It, at one sweep, repealed the whole of the common law respecting the relations of master and servant. Soon after it passed, disturbances and acts of violence took place in different parts of the country; and it became absolutely necessary to pass some act on the subject before the session closed. . . .

> This bill not only prevented the combination of workmen against masters, and of masters against workmen, but prevented the combination of workmen against workmen. This was a protection which the honest and good workman had a right to expect. The bill repealed the act of the last session; but in doing so, it also repealed the old restrictive statutes which were repealed by that act, while it restored the common law to its former state. Objection had been made to the clause for protecting workmen which contained the word 'molestation', but that was a word well known to the law, and would have a fair interpretation.

PARLIAMENTARY DEBATES, *2nd Series, vol.13, (1825) cols.1478–1479*

Peel's Work at the Home Office: 1.   Prison Reform

T.F. Buxton, a humanitarian reformer who was a product of the Evangelical movement, described the effect of imprisonment upon the prisoner in 1818:

> If convicted, beyond the sentence awarded by the law, he may be exposed to the most intolerable hardships, and these may amount to no less than the destruction of his life now, and his soul for ever. And in the violation of his rights, you equally abandon your own interest. He is instructed in no useful branch of employment by which he may earn an honest livelihood by honest labour. You have forbidden him to repent and reflect, by withholding from him every opportunity for reflection and repentance. Seclusion from the world has been only a closer intercourse with its very worst miscreants; his mind has lain waste and barren for every weed to take root in; he is habituated to idleness, reconciled to filth, and familiarised with crime. You give him leisure, and for the employment of that leisure you give him tutors in every branch of iniquity. You have taken no pious pains to turn him from the error

of his ways, and to save his soul alive. . . . In short, by the greatest possible degree of misery, you produce the greatest possible degree of wickedness; you convert an act, perhaps of indiscretion, into a settled taste and propensity to vice; receiving him, because he is too bad for society, you return him to the world impaired in health, debased in intellect, and corrupted in principles.

ENGLISH HISTORICAL DOCUMENTS, vol.11 (1783–1832)

edited by A. Aspinall and E.A. Smith   Eyre & Spottiswoode, 1969

p.385

The extent of reform as a result of the Gaols Acts of 1823, 1824 and 1825 may be judged from the later Report of a House of Commons Committee quoted below:

They have personally inspected the prisons in this metropolis and its neighbourhood, and have examined several of the visiting magistrates, chaplains, and officers of those and other prisons in various parts of the country, and whilst they have the satisfaction of believing that some of our prisons have of late been much improved, yet they cannot refrain from expressing their decided opinion that imprisonment in Newgate, Giltspur St. and the Borough Compter, in their present condition, must have the effect of corrupting the morals of their inmates, and manifestly tend to the extension rather than to the suppression of crime.

FIRST REPORT OF THE SELECT COMMITTEE OF THE HOUSE OF COMMONS ON
PRISONS   *1835*   *p.iii*

2.   The Penal Code

A long campaign had been fought by Romilly, and then Mackintosh, with little effect before Peel came to the Home Office.

From the diary of Sir Samuel Romilly:

17 Jan. 1813.   In the House of Commons I moved for leave to bring in a Bill to repeal so much of the Act of King William as punishes with death the offence of stealing privately in a shop, warehouse or stable, goods of the value of 5s. . . . I omitted the Bills formerly brought in to take away capital punishments in the cases of stealing in dwelling-houses and on board vessels, because those Bills had excited much more opposition than that relating to shops. . . .

26 March 1813.   The Bill . . . was read a third time in the Commons and passed. On the division, the numbers were, Ayes 72, Noes 34. . . .

2 April 1813.   The Bill was thrown out in the Lords today upon the second reading by a majority of 26 to 15. . . .

ENGLISH HISTORICAL DOCUMENTS, vol.11 (1783–1832)

edited by A. Aspinall and E.A. Smith   Eyre & Spottiswoode, 1959 p.392

Mackintosh managed to get this Bill, and two others, passed in 1820, but Eldon secured an amendment to keep the death penalty for stealing to the value of more than £10, and spoke against the Bill:

> While it appeared a harsh thing to condemn a man to death for stealing privately in a shop to the amount of 5s., the present bill did not provide sufficiently against the loss of property to an amount which, though it could not distress some, might effectually ruin many shopkeepers.... The apprehension of the capital punishment had deterred many from the commission of this offence.... If hereafter it should be found, that shoplifting became universal, and that many persons were reduced to misery by this crime, he hoped it would be remembered that he had suggested the consideration, whether this law which had so long existed was not wise and politic.
>
> PARLIAMENTARY DEBATES, *2nd Series, vol.2, (1820) col.493*

In 1819 Mackintosh had managed to obtain a Committee of Enquiry into the Criminal Laws, against initial Government opposition, which produced the Report on which Peel was to act. Here are two extracts from the 1819 debate:

> [Mackintosh] The criminal law is not so efficaceous as it might be, if temperate and prudent alterations were made, and if the letter of the law were more nearly assimilated to the practice, from which it has not merely deviated, but with which it is totally at variance. ... I do not call for the abolition of the punishment of death, but only for its abolition in those cases where it is very rarely and ought never to be carried into effect.
>
> [Castlereagh] He certainly was not desirous of seeing any change in the primary laws of the kingdom, unless that change operated to the improvement of morals, and to the diminution of crime.
>
> PARLIAMENTARY DEBATES, *1st Series, vol.39, (1819) cols.786–787, 796, 805*

In 1830, while opposing Mackintosh's attempt to end the death penalty for forgery, Peel justified his reform and codification of the Penal Code since coming to the Home Office.

> When he came into office seven years before the present period, the criminal law of Great Britain exceeded in severity the criminal codes of every other part of Europe, and he had then thought it ought to be meliorated. He made it, since he had been in office, the great object of his ambition, not to set the example of meliorating this code but to follow the example set by others. He had found, however, that the habits and usages of the country were adapted to and formed on the severity of our code, and he found it necessary to proceed in the mitigation of this severity with great caution. He

F

thought it advantageous to continue the severity of the law in its letter, but gradually to meliorate its practical application.

THE SPEECHES OF SIR ROBERT PEEL, vol.2 *Routledge, 1853* *p.162*

Peel summarized his work at the Home Office in 1827:
When I first entered upon the duties of the Home Department, there were laws in existence which imposed upon the subjects of this realm unusual and extraordinary restrictions; the fact is undeniable, that those laws have been effaced. Tory as I am, I have the further satisfaction of knowing, that there is not a single law connected with my name which has not had for its object some mitigation of the severity of the criminal law; some prevention of abuse in the exercise of it; or some security for its impartial administration. I may also recollect with pleasure, that during the severest trials to which the manufacturing interests have been exposed, during the winter of the last two years, I have preserved internal tranquillity, without applying to the House for measures of extraordinary severity.

MR SECRETARY PEEL
by N. Gash Longmans, 1961 *p.437*

The leading modern historian of criminal law on Peel's work:
When in 1826 Peel proclaimed his resolve to 'break the sleep of centuries' he raised high hopes. A great number of obsolete and emergency statutes were expunged and the substance of some 300 others relating to four-fifths of all offences was consolidated into four broad measures. But on the crucial issue of the severity of criminal law, and particularly the restriction of the death penalty, Peel was much behind the predominant opinion of the day. He abolished capital punishment for some minor offences against property unattended with violence, while in the words of Lord St. Leonards, 'the legislature and the country were travelling fast towards the abolition of all capital punishments.' The principle that no offence against property should be punished by death now held the field, and indeed in the course of a few ensuing years it was extended to a large group of such offences. The rapidity with which the surge of new ideas demolished Peel's legislation was remarkable.

A HISTORY OF ENGLISH CRIMINAL LAW, vol.1
by L. Radzinovicz Stevens & Sons, 1948 *pp.606–607*

London Jurors' Petition, 6 September 1831:
Your petitioners view with deep regret, the excessive and indiscriminate severity of the Criminal Laws, which annex to offences of different degrees of moral guilt the punishment of *Death*, and confound the simple invasion of the rights of property,

with the most malignant and atrocious crimes against the person and the life of man.

The recent Acts passed with the professed intention to amend and improve the Criminal Laws, have not remedied the evil of which an enlightened community have the greatest reason to complain, but have still left those laws a disgrace to our civilisation, by retaining the opprobrious distinction of being the most sanguinary of any in Europe.

A HISTORY OF ENGLISH CRIMINAL LAW, vol.1
by L. Radzinovicz   Stevens & Sons, 1948   *p.781*

Some statistics of crime and punishment:

Year	Number convicted	Sentenced to death	Executed	Executed for murder
1820	9,318	1,236	107	10
1830	12,805	1,397	46	14
1840	19,927	77	9	9

From The Progress of the Nation by G.R. Porter
quoted in PEEL, RUSSELL AND REFORM
by D.E.D. Beales   CAMBRIDGE HISTORICAL JOURNAL, vol.17,
1974   *p.879*

3. The Metropolitan Police

If a foreign jurist had then [1819] examined the condition of the metropolis, as respected crime, and the organisation of its police – and if, without tracing the circumstances from which that organisation arose, he had inferred design from the ends to which it appeared to conduce – he might have brought forward plausible reasons for believing that it was craftily framed by a body of professional depredators, upon a calculation of the best means of obtaining from society, with security to themselves, the greatest quantity of plunder. He would have found the metropolis divided and sub-divided into petty jurisdictions, each independent of every other, each having sufficiently distinct interests to engender perpetual jealousies and animosities, and being sufficiently free from any general control to prevent any intercommunity of reformation or any unity of action.

HISTORY OF THE THIRTY YEARS PEACE *1816–1846*, vol.1
by Harriet Martineau (first pub. 1858)   Bell, 1877   *p.104*

Peel's Police, formed in 1829, were unpopular at first, and not only with criminals. The Tory *Standard* newspaper attacked the scheme at the time:

Men, however prone to the graver reflections which seem to suit our times, will not fail to observe the great aptitude of the outline

STATE WATCHMEN.
OF 1829.

Wellington (left) and Peel as watchmen. The new police force is seen as militaristic, autocratic and inquisitorial, but was it so in reality?

[of the Police Book of Instructions], with all its exact arrangements of subordinate responsibility beginning in mere mechanical obedience at bottom, and ending in mere will at top FOR A PERFECT DESPOTISM. ...

The New Police is not similar to, but worse than, the gendarmerie [of France]. It is professedly a corps of spies ...

wholly repugnant to the spirit of English law and to the theory of a free government.... We would much prefer even an actual military police, with red coats and bright muskets.... The profession of a soldier has something honourable about it. Soldiers never would be spies. ... The thing is not – never was English.

BRITISH POLICE AND THE DEMOCRATIC IDEAL
by C. Reith   O.U.P., 1943   *p.53*

This handbill appeared at the time of the London riots of November 1830:

Liberty or Death! Englishmen! Britons!! and Honest Men!!! The time has at length arrived. All London meets on Tuesday. Come armed. We assure you from ocular demonstrations that 6,000 cutlasses have been removed from the Tower, for the use of Peel's Bloody Gang. Remember the cursed speech from the Throne! These damned Police are now to be armed. Englishmen will you put up with this?

BRITISH POLICE AND THE DEMOCRATIC IDEAL
by C. Reith   O.U.P., 1943   *pp.70–71*

Within a few years, however, the 'Peelers' had gained acceptance and respect:

The vast diminution in the amount of crime committed in town, and the great addition to the number of cases in which the offenders were detected, taken into custody, and prosecuted to conviction, soon became sufficiently apparent to remove gradually the prejudices so strongly and generally entertained against the new force, and to make it popular with the public. The experience of nine years has confirmed the predictions of good from it, made by the authors of the measure. Person and property are now incomparably safer than they were under the old system. The new police are now the objects of universal approbation, and most deservedly so. ... The integrity and trustworthiness of the new police, considered as a body, are above all praise.

From Sketches in London by J. Grant, 1838

quoted in NINETEENTH-CENTURY CRIME: PREVENTION AND PUNISHMENT
by J.J. Tobias   David & Charles, 1972   *p.117*

The Repeal of the Test and Corporation Acts and Catholic Emancipation. Why did the Tories disintegrate so rapidly after the retirement of Liverpool?

William Ponsonby (a Whig) wrote to Caroline Lamb about Liverpool's illness, on 20 February 1827:

Everything continues in an extraordinary state, and great anxiety is felt to know what will be the consequence. Lord Liverpool is alive, but that is all, and Canning far from strong. His party and the Duke of Wellington's, having been long held together by Lord Liverpool alone, must sever.

WELLINGTON, vol. 2 (PILLAR OF STATE)
by E. Longford   Weidenfeld & Nicolson, 1972   *p.132*

Greville commented on Canning's succession to the Premiership on 13 April 1827:

Although Canning has gained his point – has got the power into his hands and is nominally P.M. – no man ever took office under such humiliating circumstances or was placed in a more difficult and uncertain situation. ... He must form a Cabinet full of disunion, and he is doubtful what support he can expect from the old adherents of Government, by whom he is abhorred.

THE GREVILLE MEMOIRS, vol. I
edited by Lytton Strachey and Roger Fulford   Macmillan, 1938   p.172

After Canning's death and the brief Ministry headed by Goderich (Robinson), Wellington formed an unstable Government in January 1828, with Peel as Leader of the Commons.

Peel will find it quite impossible to calculate on a majority on any one question, except perhaps a motion for turning them out or reforming the Parliament, and how he is even to get thro' the forms of debate, if he is opposed by all the parties not in office, seems inconceivable. ... The Ultras [the extreme Tories] are in great force, and the Huskissons [Liberal Tories] full of faction.

THE CREEVEY PAPERS, vol.2
edited by Sir Herbert Maxwell   Murray, 1903   pp.146–147

The repeal of the Test and Corporation Acts, for which the nonconformists were pressing, was brought forward by the up-and-coming young Whig, Russell, in 1828:

The great principle, involved in the numerous petitions before the House ... signed by the whole body of Dissenters, by Roman Catholics, and by many members of the established church ... is, that every man ... should be at liberty to worship God according to the dictates of his conscience, without being subjected to any penalty or disqualification whatsoever. ... History will not justify you in maintaining these acts. ... The Dissenters of the present day feel nothing but loyalty towards the House of Hanover. ... All ground of necessity fails, the acts having been suspended for more than three quarters of a century. ... The abrogation of such laws ... will be more consonant to the tone and spirit of the age. ...

PARLIAMENTARY DEBATES, *2nd Series, vol.18, (1828) cols.678, 692–693*

Lord Ellenborough, the Lord Privy Seal, recorded the Government's initial attitude, which they abandoned when Russell's motion for repeal was carried in the Commons.

> 25 February 1828.   Cabinet at 3. Decided that the repeal of the Test and Corporation Acts should be opposed by the Government on the grounds that there was no practical inconvenience, that the thing worked well, and that it was unwise to change the relative position of persons who went on so well together. Huskisson, others, and I said we must object to the repeal, not only on that ground, but as prejudicing the Catholic question.
>
> LORD ELLENBOROUGH'S POLITICAL DIARY 1828–1830, vol.1
> *edited by Lord Colchester   Bentley, 1881*   pp.39–40

The problem of Catholic Emancipation had bedevilled English politics ever since the Act of Union with Ireland in 1800. It had influenced the composition of the Ministry in 1812, as Liverpool reminded the King on 10 November 1826:

> It was then deemed impracticable to constitute an administration upon the exclusive Protestant principle, and Your Majesty was advised by Lord Liverpool and by others, to agree to an understanding, by which the Roman Catholic question (as it was called) was no longer to be considered as a question of government, but that Your Majesty's servants, and all persons in office, should be at liberty to take the course in Parliament upon it which they might think proper, according to their own individual opinions.
>
> THE LIFE OF LORD LIVERPOOL, vol.3
> *by C.D. Yonge   Macmillan, 1868*   p.435

Emancipation motions came up in the Commons every year, and sometimes were passed, but until 1829 ministers' opposition in the Lords always secured their ultimate defeat. Liverpool summed up the 'anti-Catholic' case in 1819:

> The main objects of the Catholics were to be allowed to sit in Parliament, in the privy council, and to be eligible to the great offices of the state.... The principle of the constitution as established in 1688, was essentially Protestant; the connexion of a church and a limited monarchy was absolutely essential to the existence of civil liberty and of constitutional government; and in deciding the question that the King must be Protestant, they had also decided that the government must be Protestant likewise....
>
> The Roman Catholic not only brought a qualified allegiance, but differed from other dissenters in this, that he not only questioned the King's supremacy, but acknowledged a foreign one.... It was not true ... that the church of Rome exercised no power except in matters purely ecclesiastical. ... There could be little doubt that if the Catholic Hierarchy possessed the power,

TERRORS of EMANCIPATION – or – A Bugabo for Old Women and Children

This drawing supports the views of Wellington and Peel (on the left) over Catholic Emancipation, and ridicules the fears of their opponents such as Eldon (holding an anti-Catholic petition), the Duke of Cumberland and the Duke of Newcastle (right). Was the Irish Catholic threat no more than a 'Bugabo' or bugbear, as this suggests?

they would use that power in pursuit of farther objects, namely, for the attainment of at least a participation of the property enjoyed by the clergy of the established church. . . .

It was said that the grant of such power as was at present required would serve to produce tranquillity and harmony in Ireland. In his opinion, however, he could not acquiesce. For he could not comprehend how the Catholics were to be contented with merely that quantum of power which their advocates at present demanded. . . . Instead of producing harmony and peace, the proposed concession would rather serve to give birth to a perpetual contest between the Catholic population and the priesthood on the one hand, and the Protestant proprietors and friends of the Protestant establishment on the other, especially with regard to the possessions of the church.

PARLIAMENTARY DEBATES, *1st Series, vol.40, (1819) cols.433–438*

The case for Emancipation summarized by *The Annual Register*, 1828:
The removal of the disabilities was claimed as matter of right, unless some strong ground of expediency could be established

against them, and the existence of any such ground of expediency was denied. They had been originally imposed when everything was to be dreaded from a Catholic prince concealed or avowed; nothing was now to be dreaded, from a royal family which, by the necessity of the Constitution, must be Protestant. They had been imposed to guard against danger from the Pope and a pretender; now a pretender no longer existed, and the Pope was impotent. There was nothing in the Roman Catholic religion, to disqualify its professors from holding power in a Catholic country; for their allegiance to the Pope regarded only their faith; to persecution they were not inclined, for the spirit of popery had changed and been mitigated; and, even if they should attempt to persecute, the attempt would be futile in a Protestant country.

Above all, it was absolutely necessary to grant the demands of the Catholics; because otherwise the Catholics would not allow Ireland to enjoy a moment's repose, and, exposing us every moment to the danger of rebellion, would render that part of the

Compare this anti-Catholic cartoon with the previous illustration. Eldon (left) is Hamlet, while Peel (taking off an orange waistcoat) and Wellington are the gravediggers of the Constitution. While O'Connell (to the right of the Pope) and his Irish followers take over St. Paul's, York Minster is in flames and George IV departs for Hanover (right).

United Kingdom – what, indeed, it already was – the source of alarm, of discord, of expensive compulsory government in peace, and, in war, a source of positive weakness. It was added, that the concession was due, as being the consummation in the hope of which alone the people of Ireland had been brought to consent to the Union.

After securing the defeat of Emancipation in 1828, why did Wellington's Ministry pass it in 1829? Peel, the leader of the 'anti-Catholics', explained why he had changed his mind in a confidential memorandum to Wellington, 11 August 1828, soon after O'Connell's election for County Clare:

> I have uniformly opposed what is called Catholic Emancipation, and have rested my opposition upon broad and uncompromising grounds.
>
> I wish I could say that my views upon the question were materially changed, and that I now believed that full concessions to Roman Catholics could be made either exempt from the dangers which I have apprehended from them, or productive of the full advantages which their advocates anticipate from the grant of them.
>
> But whatever may be my opinion upon those points, I cannot deny that the state of Ireland under existing circumstances is most unsatisfactory; that it becomes necessary to make your choice between different kinds and different degrees of evil – to compare the actual danger, resulting from this union and organisation of the Roman Catholic body, and the incessant agitation in Ireland, with prospective and apprehended dangers to the constitution or religion of the country, and maturely to consider whether it may not be better to encounter every eventual risk of concession than to submit to the certain continuance, or rather perhaps the certain aggravation, of existing evils.

SIR ROBERT PEEL, vol.2

by C.S. Parker   John Murray, 1891   *p.55*

A Whig view of the Emancipation Act:

> The truth is, that the Duke was driven to the great step he so unexpectedly took, by the mere force of circumstances. ... There are two classes of Tories – those who cannot quit their places, and those who will not quit their principles. To the former he owed his majorities in favour of that question. ... The question was carried in the Commons by near two to one, – where it had never been carried before but by some half-dozen of majority. In the Lords, where it had been uniformly defeated two to one, it was carried by a large majority.

Cobbett found the 1829 Act mean and inadequate:

> The measure of 'Catholic Emancipation', as it has been ridi-
> culously, and still is ridiculously, called, has really made the state
> of the county worse than it was before, and worse than it would
> now have been, had not that measure been adopted. ... Every man
> of sense will ask, how several millions of wretched people, several
> millions of creatures half-naked and half-starved, should be raised
> into comfort and content by a mere sharing of the lay, legislative
> and executive powers between Protestants and Catholics, without
> any change whatsoever in the principles upon which those powers
> are executed, or in the manner or price of the execution?
>
> *COBBETT'S POLITICAL REGISTER, 29 August 1829*

Having alienated both the 'liberal' and the 'ultra Tories', Wellington
was now in a precarious position, and he lacked the tact and political
skill to get out of it. A Whig M.P. described the situation in the
Commons in June 1830:

> Ministers have no secure majority, for whenever the old Oppo-
> sition and the ultras can agree on any subject, they must be left in a
> minority. The Duke of Wellington has certainly done more for the
> country than any former Minister, but it is not enough to meet the
> necessities of the times; the country begins to be tired of his
> despotism.
>
> ENGLISH RADICALISM 1786–1832
> *by S. Maccoby   Allen & Unwin, 1955*   *p.426*

Two further issues now brought Wellington's Ministry to its fall. The
first was the economic depression of 1829–1830, as Greville noted:

> The country gentlemen are ... all of the same story as to the
> universally prevailing distress and the certainty of things becom-
> ing much worse; of the failure of rents all over England, and the
> necessity of some decisive measures or the prospect of general
> ruin. ... It really does appear, from many representations, that a
> notion prevails of the Duke of Wellington's indifference to the
> state of the country, and of his disposition to treat the re-
> monstrances and petitions of the people, as well as their interests
> and feelings, with contempt, which I believe to be most false and
> unjust. He has an overweening opinion of his own all-sufficiency,
> and that is his besetting sin, and the one which, if anything does,
> will overturn his Government; for if he would be less dictatorial
> and opinionated, and would call to his assistance such talents and
> information as the crisis demands, he would be universally voted
> the best man alive to be at the head of the Government.
>
> THE GREVILLE MEMOIRS, vol. I
> *edited by Lytton Strachey and Roger Fulford, Macmillan, 1938 pp. 358–359*

Wellington failed to strengthen his Ministry, and after the General Election necessitated by the death of George IV, which weakened rather than strengthened his Parliamentary position, he sealed his fate with his speech on Parliamentary Reform on 2 November 1830.

> He had never read or heard of any measure up to the present moment which could in any degree satisfy his mind that the state of the representation could be improved.... He was fully convinced that the country possessed at the present moment a legislature which answered all the good purposes of legislation, and this to a greater degree than any legislature ever had answered in any country what ever. He would go further and say, that the legislature and the system of representation possessed the full and entire confidence of the country. ...
>
> The representation of the people at present contained a large body of the property of the country, in which the landed interest had a preponderating influence. Under these circumstances, ... he was not only not prepared to bring forward any measure [of parliamentary reform], but he would at once declare that as far as he was concerned, as long as he held any station in the government of the country, he should always feel it his duty to resist such measures when proposed by others.
>
> PARLIAMENTARY DEBATES, *3rd Series, vol.1, (1830) cols.52–53*

Within a fortnight the Government had been defeated in the Commons and resigned. The *Edinburgh Review* summed up the events of 1830:

> The ambitious but short-sighted conduct of the Duke of Wellington ... was consummated by his dissolving the Parliament, and appealing to the country [this was necessitated by the death of George IV], in the forlorn state in which he and his colleagues had been exhibited during the last session. The results of the general election were fatal to whatever remained of strength in his Cabinet; and all men foresaw that a change must needs be made, either by his at length consenting to share his power with those in whom the country and the Parliament reposed confidence, or by his being driven entirely from office, with his adherents. ... But what no soothsayer could have foretold, was the extraordinary series of blunders by which the Duke's fall was precipitated. It may very safely be affirmed, that the whole history of administrations in ordinary times ... will be in vain ransacked for any parallel. ...
>
> THE *EDINBURGH REVIEW*, vol.52   *1831*   *p.531*

Mrs. Arbuthnot, the Duke's confidante, took a different view:

> During the three years of his Government he has relieved the Catholics and the Dissenters, he has cut down the estimates *many millions*, he has put every possible office down as they become vacant, he has taken off above three millions of taxes, he, in

conjunction with Peel, has improved the police, simplified the laws; in short, in three years he has introduced great and substantial reforms and, because he will not play tricks with the Constitution and give more power to the democrats than they ought to have, he is hooted and abused and driven from the helm.

MRS ARBUTHNOT'S DIARY, vol.2

edited by Francis Bamford and the Duke of Wellington   Macmillan, 1950

p.403

A recent historian gives this estimate of the 'liberal Tories':

'Liberal Toryism' of the 1820s . . . was the resultant of many forces whose stability was precarious. . . . The leaders of the Tories were much more liberal than most of their Parliamentary supporters, and also much more aware of public opinion. . . . The King and the House of Lords were firmly against 'fundamental' reform. By comparison with what had gone before, the measures of the Administration between 1822 and 1827 seem notably liberal and reformist. By comparison with what followed, they seem merely trivial tinkering. . . . Nothing serious could be done about the Church. Slavery could not be abolished. It is significant that it was in foreign policy that liberalism seemed most pronounced. It is significant also that even here there was a greater change of style than of substance. But the respectable public was temporarily satisfied that reform could proceed without constitutional change.

FROM CASTLEREAGH TO GLADSTONE

by D.E.D. Beales   Nelson, 1969   *p.82*

By 1830 the public was no longer satisfied. The 'liberal Tories' had not proved liberal enough, the 'ultra Tories' remained strong, and the men who had come to see the government of England as theirs by right finally fell before the renewed and rapidly growing demand for Parliamentary Reform. In the struggle against the Whig Reform Bills, old Toryism was destroyed as a major political force, and out of the debacle was born, under the leadership of Peel and the 'liberal Tory' remnant, the new Conservative Party, though still retaining a substantial Tory right wing which was to bring down Peel in turn in 1846. But old Toryism never governed England again.

Further Reading

D.E.D. Beales   *From Castlereagh to Gladstone 1815–1885*   (NELSON, 1969)

I. Bradley   *The Call to Seriousness* (on Evangelicalism)   (CAPE, 1976)

A. Brady   *William Huskisson and Liberal Reform*   (O.U.P., 1928)

A. Briggs   *The Age of Improvement 1783–1867*   (LONGMANS, 1958)

W.R. Brock   *Lord Liverpool and Liberal Toryism*   (C.U.P., 1941)

J.E. Cookson   *Lord Liverpool's Administration 1815–1822*   (SCOTTISH ACADEMIC PRESS, 1975)

T.A. Critchley   *A History of the Police in England and Wales*   (CONSTABLE, 1967)

S. Maccoby   *English Radicalism 1786–1832*   (ALLEN & UNWIN, 1955)

G.I.T. Machin   *The Catholic Question in English Politics*   (O.U.P., 1964)

P. Mathias   *The First Industrial Nation*   (METHUEN, 1969)

A. Mitchell   *The Whigs in Opposition 1815–1830*   (O.U.P., 1967)

H. Perkin   *The Origins of Modern English Society 1780–1880*   (ROUTLEDGE, 1972)

D. Read   *Peterloo*   (MANCHESTER U. P., 1958)

E.P. Thompson   *The Making of the English Working Class* (PENGUIN, 1968)

H. van Thal (editor)   *The Prime Ministers*, vol. 1   (ALLEN & UNWIN, 1974)

R.J. White   *Waterloo to Peterloo* (PENGUIN, 1968)

Biographies

J.W. Derry   *Castlereagh*   (ALLEN LANE, 1976)

J.W. Derry   *The Radical Tradition*   (MACMILLAN, 1967)

P. Dixon   *Canning*   (WEIDENFELD & NICOLSON, 1976)

N. Gash   *Mr Secretary Peel*   (LONGMANS, 1961)

J.F.C. Harrison   *Robert Owen and the Owenites*   (ROUTLEDGE, 1969)

C. Hibbert   *George IV, Regent and King*   (PENGUIN, 1976)

W.D. Jones   *Prosperity Robinson*   (MACMILLAN, 1967)

E. Longford   *Wellington: Pillar of State*   (WEIDENFELD & NICOLSON, 1972)

J.W. Osborne *William Cobbett: His Thought and his Time* (RUTGERS U. P., 1966)

P. Ziegler *Addington* (COLLINS, 1965)

Diaries

Francis Bamford and the Duke of Wellington (editors) *Mrs Arbuthnot's Journal*, vols. 1 and 2 (MACMILLAN, 1950)

Lytton Strachey and Roger Fulford (editors) *The Greville Memoirs*, vols. 1 and 2 (MACMILLAN, 1938)

Documents

A. Aspinall and E.A. Smith (editors) *English Historical Documents*, vol. 11 (*1783–1832*) (EYRE & SPOTTISWOODE, 1959)

D. Holman (editor) *Portraits and Documents: the earlier nineteenth century* (HUTCHINSON, 1965)

E.R. Pike (editor) *Human Documents of the Industrial Revolution in Britain* (ALLEN & UNWIN, 1967)

Acknowledgments
and Sources

pages 6, 13, 19, 29, 31, 39, 43, 45, 48, 51, 53, 54, 59, 72, 76, & 77 — Illustrations by George Cruikshank reproduced by Courtesy of the Trustees of the British Museum

pages 9, 21, & 56 — Illustrations by George Cruikshank reproduced by Courtesy of Mary Evans Picture Library

pages 11, 15, 17, 18, 20, 23, & 24 — National Portrait Gallery, London

page 8 — Portrait of *The Prince Regent in Garter Robes* by Sir Thomas Lawrence reproduced by gracious permission of Her Majesty the Queen